METAMORPHOSIS

WAYNE T. HUDSON SR.

CREATION HOUSE
H O U S E
A STRANG COMPANY

METAMORPHOSIS by Wayne Hudson
Published by Creation House
A Strang Company
600 Rinehart Road
Lake Mary, Florida 32746
www.strangbookgroup.com

Unless otherwise noted, all Scripture quotations are from the Holy Bible, New International Version of the Bible. Copyright © 1973, 1978, 1984, International Bible Society. Used by permission.

Scripture quotations marked KJV are from the King James Version of the Bible.

Scripture quotations marked NKJV are from the New King James Version of the Bible. Copyright © 1979, 1980, 1982 by Thomas Nelson, Inc., publishers. Used by permission.

Design Director: Bill Johnson
Cover design by Justin Evans
Cover photo by Dick Madden

Library of Congress Control Number: 2009943072
International Standard Book Number: 978-1-61638-144-8

First Edition

10 11 12 13 14 — 9 8 7 6 5 4 3 2 1
Printed in the United States of America

DEDICATION

THIS BOOK IS dedicated to God first. He is my best friend and greatest ally, and it is my desire to serve Him first and foremost.

This book is dedicated to my wife, Goldie, who has stood by my side since February 27, 1971. She has supported my every endeavor, whether it has been for her, our family, our God, or our country. She has been invaluable to me all these years and has labored alongside me in producing this book for its intended use and purpose.

This book is dedicated to my parents, Tom and Alice Hudson, who raised me in the fear and admonition of the Lord.

This book is dedicated to my three loving children, Wayne Jr. or "Tommy," Timothy, and Terran, and all of my precious grandchildren, because without their love and admiration I would never have had the confidence to tackle such a project.

The book is dedicated to all those who are enduring times of trouble. God has promised that He will never leave you or forsake you. Through every moment of every day, He is right by your side. My prayer is that this book will be an inspiration to you and a source of information, guidance, and help in focusing and prioritizing in the future!

CONTENTS

PREFACE

I WANT TO THANK every person that began the Tea Party movement or participated by attending the rallies or doing anything else to help; you began the big tent revival of 2010. You kicked it off! My new Republican hat is off to you.

The 9.12 Project is equally responsible with their organization and rallies. You folks have all done an excellent job, and I will forever be grateful to you for the momentum you have established.

You folks are the sparks that set the fire off in the wet kindling. We have heard you loud and clear and welcome you to the party—the Republican Party with the "big tent"!

The firstfruits of your efforts were realized on November 3, 2009, with the victory in the Commonwealth of Virginia. What an outpouring. That is truly a blessing! The second victory was in the north with the win in New Jersey. See what We the People can do when we are united? This revival is now spreading like wildfire. I firmly believe if we maintain this momentum and unity with the marvelous Independents helping, voting, and cheering all of us on, the revival under the "big tent" will continue to every state in the Union, the good Lord willing.

Believe it or not, I wrote the preceding before I read my devotion for today, 2 Corinthians 3:6: "He has made us competent as ministers of a new covenant—not of the letter but of the Spirit; for the letter kills, but the Spirit gives life."

I guess you could say I'm a little like Hannity except I'm a registered Republican; I'm a Christian first; I'm a 9.12 social conservative; and last but not least, I'm a conservationist who has strong beliefs in God, country, and energy independence!

We are the envy of the world. The biggest thing we need is ordained leadership and better coaching, and we make no apologies!

I can't stress the importance of the next elections enough. It's going to be the fight and battle of our lives. If we can't at least reverse the situation in the Senate, I believe we will have kissed our freedom good-bye! We are at the biggest crossroads of our lives and the life of our country!

ACKNOWLEDGMENTS

I WANT TO ACKNOWLEDGE and thank Dr. Lester M. Sitzes, III, for being used in a mighty way to give me some direction, information, and most of all encouragement when I was just beginning to collect information and data for this book.

Thanks also to Strang Communications and the Creation House team.

INTRODUCTION

ONE OF THE reasons I began writing this book was to help me decide if I want to change my voter registration to "Republican" or "Independent." I decided after fourteen chapters of writing, analyzing, and researching, that although the Republican Party is far from perfect, it is still the best we have! It's my party because it's the best. It has the potential for being near perfect if we would all get behind it, forget our petty differences, and make it the best it can be!

I was raised in a small town in rural north Florida at the crossroads of I-75 and I-10, just thirty-five miles north of Gator country! Lake City is still under eleven thousand in population, while Columbia County weighs in at approximately seventy-five thousand, depending on whom you ask.

Most people have historically registered as Democrats in this area to be able to have a say in local government (i.e., school superintendent, school board, county commission, etc.), because most people who have run for these offices and have been elected have been Democrats. This is changing now, and with what the Democratic Party has become, I'm embarrassed for anyone to know I was as of recently still registered as one, as none of my beliefs coincide with the Democratic platform! It's almost anti-religion now, it seems, and I'm an ordained Baptist deacon.

I'm hearing a lot these days that the Republican Party

is down, ashamed, looking for answers, examining people's ideas for the party, and trying to decide if the size and shape of their umbrella is right. (There is nothing wrong with a critical exam!) I believe the party is just right to go forward, with a few exceptions. The platform is basically Bible-based, and you can't go wrong with that. As time goes on, this is going to become increasingly more important, because our country was founded on biblical principles.

The biblical order for our country in these perilous times in our land begins, "If my people, who are called by my name, will humble themselves and pray and seek my face and turn from their wicked ways, then will I hear from heaven and will forgive their sin and will heal their land" (2 Chron. 7:14). Seems like a simple solution to me!

The few exceptions I would like to see worked into the Republican Party platform are:

- Consider a party name change or be known as something such as "The People's Party."
- More pride in who we are and what we stand for!

Apparently folks do not realize that the Republican Party's ideology fits close to the letter of intent stated by the 9.12 Project, as follows:

THE NINE PRINCIPLES

1. America is good.
2. I believe in God and He is the Center of my Life.
3. I must always try to be a more honest person than I was yesterday.

4. The family is sacred. My spouse and I are the ultimate authority, not the government.
5. If you break the law you pay the penalty. Justice is blind and no one is above it.
6. I have a right to life, liberty, and the pursuit of happiness, but there is no guarantee of equal results.
7. I work hard for what I have and I will share it with whom I want to. Government cannot force me to be charitable.
8. It is not un-American for me to disagree with authority or to share my personal opinion.
9. The government works for me. I do not answer to them, they answer to me.[1]

THE TWELVE VALUES

1. Honesty
2. Reverence
3. Hope
4. Thrift
5. Humility
6. Charity
7. Sincerity
8. Moderation
9. Hard Work
10. Courage
11. Personal Responsibility
12. Gratitude[2]

I am only a registered voter and member of the party, but I want to be one of the first to make a motion that we accept the 9.12 Project's principles and values as clarifications to our ideology. Perhaps I'm missing something, but I believe most Republicans believe in these principles and values. It seems to me the 9.12 Project's objective simply helps clarify our long-time stated positions on God and country, the right to life, the marriage amendment, family values, capitalism, etc. I certainly do not have a problem with clarifying all of our ideals. I do not see any reason we are not already unified. After all, our strength comes from unity. Our founding fathers had the right idea; our Constitution's preamble begins with, "We the people."

Don't look back at the '06 and '08 races; they are over. Be proud you were not embarrassed at the polls, considering Obama had unlimited foreign funding. (This should be investigated.) McCain made several serious mistakes, such as denouncing support from two of America's most evangelical leaders. McCain's running mate was courageous, but the liberal news media is still having a heyday over her. The Independent voters dug in two weeks before the election and decided that because of McCain's age they could not vote for him in such times.

There are some tedious tasks I feel the Republican Party should be working toward now for the future. For one, their candidate offering should be matched together with their platform and ideology instead of drafting candidates who have a history of flip-flopping on moral issues to run as Republicans.

At least we can be proud Rudy Giuliani was who he was

and is and didn't lie or change back and forth depending on where he was at the time. It is my understanding that another leading candidate, a former governor of Massachusetts, Mitt Romney, had a history of flip-flopping on issues and did not have a fit record to run on! You really need to check this record. When running for governor of Massachusetts, Romney opposed the Federal Marriage Amendment and promised homosexuals that he would do more for them than Teddy Kennedy, as well as supporting gay rights, abortion, and stiff gun control![3] Why would a person want to run on the Republican platform if they do not believe in it? Because they can't get anywhere running as an Independent? To get elected at any cost? For power?

I have nothing personal against Romney, but history speaks. A person's past projects his future. One bright spot about Mr. Romney is that you hear people say he has proven skills in financial management. It is my understanding this came from his coming in and taking over some form of management of the Olympics, and by doing so he kept the Olympics from showing a loss. Whoa! All you would need to do is make a phone call and get some associates to bail it out.

I'll bet Obama probably could get some of his associates to bail our government out with a phone call. I'll also bet you we would not want him to! We make no apologies. After one term his state became a nightmare financially, yet he has most people believing he is some kind of financial whiz. This should be a lesson in being careful whom you trust. Check the record yourself. The state-run healthcare program he began is still a disaster!

The Republican Party needs to push laws forward in each state that would regulate the news media prejudices. The liberal news media is running and ruining this country as much as the Democrats. They remind me of communist-owned and communist-controlled news agencies. We need to find ways to nip it in the bud, such as instituting fines on airtime or on press releases that are not honestly reporting the news without prejudice. Another option would be to institute fines when the time given for each candidate is not fair and equal. Failure to change the way the liberal news media runs things is quickly preventing qualified people from becoming a part of government service.

Because of the difference in the size of the Republican Party as compared to the Democratic Party—42 percent to low 30 percent—it would behoove Republican Party leaders to give more consideration to the will of the Independent-registered voter. We would not have to water down our message or change our ideology to do so.

We could do this by polling. For example, after the Republicans have, say, three similar contestants in a Republican contest for president, these names could be presented to Independents in a private poll so they could rate each candidate according to their preferences in several categories. The information gleaned from this could help unify the Republican voters behind not just the candidates with the most-recognized name or the most popularity, but behind those who might be considered the most "electable" by Independents. Let's face it; we need their help. We may never win without the strong support of Independents.

If no other message is valued in this entire book, I hope this one will settle in and make a huge statement: Republican-registered voters and Independent-registered voters have a lot in common. In particular, neither group is likely to elect anyone or succeed at anything without the help of the other. In old Florida, southern talk, I call this "working smarter instead of harder" for a likely defeat again by guess who.

Also, if possible, consideration should be given to the way the vice presidential candidate is selected. The presidential nominee candidate may have the final say, but Republican constituents and Independents should be polled about their preferences to determine the potential vice presidential candidate's electability.

I want to urge people of all faiths, races, and ages to consider being active in the Republican Party! I believe every person who believes in God, His Word, and that He is coming back for us again could be reasonably happy in this party. Remember, there is strength in numbers and victory with unity!

Star Parker, a freelance writer and president of the Coalition on Urban Renewal and Education (CURE), states some related opinions so eloquently.

> The Republican Party is supposedly deader than a doornail, except in a handful of states in mid-America and in the South. Americans, according to these columnists, see Republicans as insolvent, out of touch, mean spirited dinosaurs. And, they continue, among those groups that will demographically define the America of tomorrow—the under-30 crowd and non-white America—Republicans are toast.

These many columns inevitably lead to the conclusion that Republicans have no choice but to lighten up on the conservative agenda and buy into a new America of big government and gay marriage.

But, may I remind folks that we just had a presidential election in which 130 million voters cast ballots and that the difference between the winner and the loser was nine million votes. Not exactly what I would call an insurmountable divide.

Nor should we forget that there was that window following the Republican Convention when the McCain–Palin ticket was leading.

A new Wall Street Journal/NBC poll shows forty-two percent self-identifying as Democrats compared to thirty-one percent as Republicans. But the same poll shows thirty-five percent identifying as conservative compared to twenty-four percent as liberals.

According to Dick Polman of the Philadelphia Inquirer, Arlen Spector's switch to the Democratic Party shows what's wrong with Republicans—they can't tolerate moderates—and not what is wrong with Spector.

But there is little doubt that Spector changed parties because polls were showing him getting his clock cleaned in the Republican Primary by conservative, Pat Toomey.

More revealing about Spector is that in light of this, he didn't simply choose to retire...

Truth is that Spector is neither a Republican nor a Democrat. He is a self serving egotist that stands for nothing other than the pursuit of personal political power and having the federal government as his sand box to play in...

The party's future lies in principles not in pandering. We need George Washingtons not Arlen Spectors.[4]

one

MY CURIOSITY WITH HOPE
AND ITS LEADERS

Photo credit: Division of Parks and Tourism, Hope, Arkansas

PLEASE EXCUSE ME if you feel my writing is not the writing of a professional. I'm sure it isn't, because I've never written a book before. But I sure am having fun.

I had been challenged in my daily devotions during early April to get focused in certain areas of the Master's work. You become effective by being selective. It's human nature to get distracted. We're like gyroscopes, spinning around at frantic paces but not getting anywhere. Without a clear purpose you keep changing jobs, directions, relationships, churches, etc., hoping each change will settle the confusion or fill the emptiness in your heart, in your life. You think this time it will be different, but it does not solve your real problem—lack of focus.

As a response to that challenge, I began writing. I felt a unique calling early in the morning of April 15, 2009, to write this book—write what I saw, heard, and felt in my quest to make an informed decision about how to register as a voter and satisfy my curiosity about some other topics along the way. (It seems I'm feeling like sharing the thoughts I'm having in retirement with the whole world. I hope you don't mind. I'll try to keep it short and as inoffensive as possible!)

Since the first time I heard of Bill Clinton, then the governor of Arkansas, I have been intrigued about his birthplace in Hope, Arkansas. This curiosity, if you please, has only multiplied over the years, especially with hearing that Governor Mike Huckabee was also from there. Is it the community; the climate; the schools; a particular, different spiritual climate; or maybe even the water? I understand the water comes from very deep wells with consistently high quality. I wonder if the water sneaks through the aquifer from Hot Springs on its way to Hope. Or the town may be doubly blessed at the nearby active diamond mines. Whatever the reason two famous politicians came from that same place, I knew that one day when I retired I would go to Hope and see for myself!

What's different about these two men born in Hope,

Arkansas? What is their hope? What is our hope and the hope of our country? This is what we will be exploring in this entire book. Metamorphosis is what we have had going on for the past sixteen years, what is going on now, and what will be happening in the future.

A lot of us consider ourselves evangelicals. This usually means we are serious Christians and generally conservative on political issues. There are approximately 70 to 80 million of us in the United States![1] However, about 24 million of us are not registered to vote, and only about 20 to 25 percent of the Christians in America vote in U.S. elections.[2] The results from these staggering numbers are as follows: nine out of ten new Congressman elected in 2006 opposed the right to life and the marriage amendment![3]

We have not seen the figures for the 2008 elections as yet, but they are probably equally dismal. One reason being, there was not a lot of excitement about our Republican presidential nominee, who foolishly, in my opinion, disavowed two of our most prominent evangelicals' support.

Also, there was a lot of confusion as to who the true evangelical candidates really were. Obama claimed to be one, even with his stand on abortion. He disavowed his pastor and church beliefs of over twenty years, even before the election. Even a couple of the Republican candidates were flip-flopping all over the place about their beliefs on abortion and other issues. (They just wanted to buy your vote, if possible.)

One bright hope we have is that statistics prove that we can make a difference if we unite for a cause. In the 2004 elections, eight out of ten new Congressmen elected were pro-life. So you can see what evangelicals can accomplish when they are united about their candidate. If he/she truly is a believer, the numbers would be unbeatable, particularly with God on our side. However, we still need a much larger percentage to register and vote for true evangelical candidates! Voting is a privilege, it is a right, and it is a necessity. It seems more obvious now that it is the only way to maintain our freedom.

John Hagee states that we can turn negative trends in America around and turn our country back to God by being concerned and active. In Luke 19:13, Jesus commands us to stay occupied until He comes.

In his book *Do the Right Thing* Mike Huckabee states that we are to persevere and keep our surroundings from spoiling! We are to initiate action: act like salt and save the world. Concerning light, a believer who covers his light does not value life very much. His light has to be uncovered. This is of utmost importance, considering the perilous times in which we live.

Below is a funny but on-point story I read recently called "Presidential Kittens."

A pretty little girl named Suzy was standing on the sidewalk in front of her home. Next to her was a basket containing a number of tiny creatures; in her hand was a sign announcing free kittens.

Suddenly a line of big black cars pulled up beside her. Out of the lead car stepped a tall, grinning man.

"Hi there little girl, I'm President Obama. What do you have in the basket?" he asked.

"Kittens," said little Suzy.

"How old are they?" asked Obama.

Suzy replied, "They're so young, their eyes aren't even open yet."

"And what kind of kittens are they?"

"Democrats," answered Suzy with a smile.

Obama was delighted. As soon as he returned to his car, he called his PR Chief and told him about the little girl and the kittens.

Recognizing the perfect photo op, the two men agreed that the President should return the next day and, in front of the assembled media, have the girl talk about her discerning kittens.

So the next day, Suzy was again standing on the sidewalk with her basket of "free kittens" when another motorcade pulled up, this time followed by vans from ABC, NBC, CBS, and CNN.

Cameras and audio equipment were quickly set up, then Obama got out of his limo and walked over to little Suzy.

"Hello again," he said, "I'd love it if you would tell all my friends out there what kind of kittens you're giving away."

"Yes sir," Suzy said. "They're Republicans."

Taken by surprise, the President stammered, "But, but, yesterday, you told me they were Democrats."

Little Suzy smiled and said, "I know, but today they have their eyes open."[4]

two

PRESIDENT BILL CLINTON

Clinton home where he lived as a baby to approximately three
years of age with grandparents in Hope, Arkansas

B ILL CLINTON HAD two best friends as a child in Hope:
Vincent Foster and Thomas "Mack" McLarty. They
not only grew up with Bill but also were a part of his
presidential administration, with McLarty being his chief of
staff. (He is presently a strong lobbyist in Washington.)

Their friendship was very close through the first grade,
including going through Miss Marie Perkins's kindergarten
class together. I mention this kindergarten, because according

16

to sources in Hope, this is the one common cord between Clinton and his buddies' education together. It is also a similarity between Mike Huckabee and his best childhood friends. They were all also trained by Miss Perkins about ten years apart! Very possibly they all attended Brookwood Elementary School, with the exception of Bill Clinton since he left town after first grade. They may have all also been born in the same hospital—Julia Chester Hospital, an old frame structure that has since been replaced by a funeral home at 1001 South Main Street.

Boyhood home of Bill Clinton, approximately four years of age to six years of age, or through first grade, Hope, Arkansas

I discovered the following in Hope, Arkansas: a brief biography of President Bill Clinton reflects that he was born William Jefferson Blythe, III, on August 19, 1946, at Julia Chester Hospital. Bill's father was killed in a car accident four months prior to Bill's birth. Bill lived with his maternal grandparents at 117 South Hervey in Hope. (This is a small two-story home located on the main street downtown. The home has been restored nicely and is advertised as Bill's home place.)

Bill's mother, Virginia Cassidy, was in school between 1946 and 1950 in New Orleans and Shreveport training to be a nurse anesthetist. In 1950, she married Roger Clinton, the owner of the Buick dealership in Hope, Arkansas. Bill's family resided at 321 East Thirteenth Street. This home has also been restored and designated as his family home in Hope.

- 1951–1952: Bill attended Mary Perkins's kindergarten on East Second Street in Hope.
- 1952–1953: Bill attended first grade at Brookwood Public School in Hope.
- Summer 1953: Bill's family moved to Hot Springs, Arkansas, where his step-father, Roger Clinton sold cars. (Bill took the Clinton name in 1961 at age fifteen.)
- 1960–1964 (high school): Bill excelled in academics, clubs, American Legion activities, and band (playing the saxophone). He enjoyed golf and would often caddy to earn extra spending money.
- 1962: Bill shook hands with President Kennedy while attending an American Legion event in Washington.
- 1964: Graduated from Hot Springs High School
- 1968: Graduated from Georgetown University
- 1969: Rhodes Scholar at Oxford University

- 1971: Graduated from Yale University Law School
- 1972: Worked in Texas for George McGovern's presidential campaign
- 1972–1976: Taught law at the University of Arkansas
- 1974: Ran for Congress and lost to the Republican incumbent representative
- 1975: Married Hillary Rodham, a Yale Law graduate from Illinois
- 1976: Elected attorney general of Arkansas
- 1978: Elected governor of Arkansas at age thirty-two, making him the youngest governor in the nation
- 1980: Daughter, Chelsea, was born in Little Rock, Arkansas, on February 17
- 1980: Voted out of office and began a law practice in Little Rock
- 1982: Bill was reelected governor of Arkansas. (During his ten years as governor he received national recognition for his education reform program.)
- 1986–1991: Bill served as chairman of the National Governor Association and chairman of the Education Commission of States. He represented the nation's governors in working with Congress to restructure the nation's welfare. He also was co-chair of the President's Education Summit to draft national education goals in 1991. He received legislative approval for a

sweeping package of improvements in education, health, environment, highways, and voca-
tional tech programs.
- 1992: Elected president of the United States on
  November 3
- 1996: Elected to his second term as president
  on November 5[1]

Remembering back, Bill Clinton ran using the motto
"It's the economy, stupid." This was successful for him and
the country, as the economy did rev up for a good five-year
period until we started sliding toward a recession in 1999.

Clinton was a good president. Compared to what we
have now, he was a saint in some ways!

One of my biggest regrets is that during his campaign
and first year as president, he really went all out to bring
homosexuals out of their closets and make them feel good
about themselves. Hollywood and Broadway followed suit
and began structuring gays and lesbians into almost every
film. It was the beginning of the largest downward spiral
and decay of moral fiber in the history of our country! Also,
somehow during Clinton's two terms, bank qualifying of
home mortgages became easy enough that almost anyone
could qualify for a bank loan. (I understand some of this
was legislated.)

During this same time period, banks all across the
country were approving high-risk mortgage applications.
This is the foundation of why we are in a crisis with foreclosures today. These foreclosures are the foundation for
Wall Street's problems, Main Street's problems, Detroit's

problems, and unemployment problems, thus resulting in the "repression" our country is involved in. I've given it a new name that fits!

These eight years when Clinton was in office, his legacy, are part of why I've titled this book *Metamorphosis*. Change did take place—change that none of us should be proud of. It could also be the beginning of the end.

As I mentioned, Clinton and Obama were already working toward lowering the mortgage standards, which is without a doubt the key ingredient to our financial collapse. Then apparently Clinton, with the aid of Hollywood and Broadway, began the march to the moral decay of our country. I sure would not be proud to have any part of this be a huge part of my legacy!

three

MIKE HUCKABEE: THE
OTHER MAN FROM HOPE

Mike Huckabee's boyhood home in Hope, Arkansas

WHILE IN HOPE, I met two of Mike Huckabee's best friends from elementary school, Tommy Holt and Lester Sitzes.

When I was fortunate enough to find Lester in his office—it seemed like divine intervention, as not much about Mike was available at the Depot Museum—he shut down his office, patients, and staff for at least thirty minutes to give me directions and to tell me about his and Mike's friendship. They had basically adopted each other as brothers in Boy Scouts, elementary school, and high school. He introduced me to his black lab, Duke. He is eight years old and is related to Mike's eleven-year-old lab, Jet. Mike had given Duke to Lester.

So Lester could get his office cranking again, he invited me to supper with their mutual friend, Tommy Holt, and they enjoyed telling me about some of the times they and Mike had together, from chasing mosquito spray trucks to many other daring feats as boys!

Mike had a sister, Pat, but no brothers. Lester and Janet, Mike's wife, grew up going to First Baptist Church of Hope and were friends. Mike attended Garrett Missionary Baptist Church with his family.

In high school, one of Mike's earliest leadership accomplishments was being elected "Governor of Arkansas Boys State." Lester and Tommy expressed that they were products of Mrs. Anna E. Williams's student government classes. "Mrs. Williams let you know that she expected great things from you," they said. Mike was president of student council during his senior year.

Mike attended Southwestern Baptist Theological Seminary in Fort Worth, Texas, and one of his classmates was Reverend Rick Warren of Saddleback Church in California. While in college Mike worked for James Robison Ministries in Texas.

My wife and I also visited the first church where Mike and Janet pastored to take some pictures, since it is located near his college campus. Although Mike was very young, he was very capable!

He and Janet were high school sweethearts and have

a daughter, Sarah, and two sons, John Mark and David. Mike and Janet duck hunt together, and most of the family graduated from Ouachita Baptist University, located in Arkadelphia, Arkansas.

Ouachita is not an average church school. It is obvious from the first minute you set foot on campus that it is all first-rate, superior, and very beautiful. My wife, Goldie, and I visited to get a feel for it and wanted to see Governor Huckabee's governorship papers, which have been filed there. Unfortunately, they had not been processed for viewing at that time.

We also took pictures of Mike's boyhood home, located on Second Street in Hope, Arkansas, and the old firehouse where his father was a career fireman. It is also located on Second Street.

Mike Huckabee's father's firehouse where he was a
career fireman, located on same street as their home

One of our most precious memories is visiting the old radio station out near Interstate 30 where Mike began his career at the age of fourteen. He was an official announcer at KXAR 1490 AM. Haskell Jones, who was a strong, well-respected Republican, was the station's general manager, and he made a strong impression on Mike from the beginning.

Mike Huckabee's first place of employment: KXAR radio station in Hope, Arkansas. He became a DJ at the age of fourteen.

To sum up this part, I was discussing some of this with an older gentleman who was at the Hope Holiday Inn Express. He said he had known Mike's father pretty well and that they were a fine family with a good reputation. He also said he was particularly proud of Mike because he had really pulled himself up.

Huckabee, fifty-four, is an avid musician and is the bass player in his rock-n-roll band, "Capital Offense," which has opened for artists such as Willie Nelson and the Charlie Daniels Band, and has played the House of Blues in New Orleans, the Red Rocks Amphitheater in Denver, Colorado, and for two presidential inauguration balls. He is featured each

week in the musical segment of his Fox Show with
the Fox house band, "The Little Rockers."[1]

In the Depot Museum in Hope, where there are several
nice displays of Mike Huckabee's past, one of them is titled
"The Other Man from Hope."

Former Arkansas governor Mike Huckabee is the
host of the number one rated weekend hit "Huckabee" on the Fox News Channel, and is heard three
times daily across the nation on the "Huckabee
Report"...

He is the author of [several] books, the most
recent being "Do the Right Thing," which spent its
first 7 weeks of release in the top ten of the New
York Times Bestseller list...

From 1996–2007, Huckabee served as the 44th
Governor of Arkansas and was recognized as a
national leader, having been honored by several
renowned publications and organizations for his
numerous accomplishments. *Governing* magazine
named him as one of its "Public Officials of the
Year" of 2005, *Time* magazine honored him as one
of the five best governors in America, and later in the
same year Huckabee received the American Association of Retired Persons' Impact Award. In 2007,
he was presented with the Music For Life Award
by the National Association of Music Merchants
(NAMM) for his commitment to music education. He served as the Chairman of the prestigious
National Governors Association as well as the

Education Commission of the States and the Interstate Oil and Gas Commission.

Huckabee became Governor in July 1996 when his predecessor resigned. He was one of the youngest governors in the country at the time. He was elected to a full four-year term as governor in 1998, attracting the largest percentage of the vote ever received by a Republican gubernatorial nominee in Arkansas, and was re-elected to another four-year term in November 2002.

He was first elected lieutenant governor in a 1993 special election and was elected to a full four-year term in 1994. He was only the fourth Republican to be elected to statewide office since Reconstruction.

A significant part of his early life was spent as a pastor and denominational leader. He became the youngest president ever of the Arkansas Baptist State Convention, the largest denomination in Arkansas. He led rapidly growing congregations in Pine Bluff and Texarkana…

Huckabee's efforts to improve his own health have received national attention. Diagnosed with Type II diabetes in 2003, he lost 110 pounds. Barely two years later, he had completed four marathons…

His hobbies include hunting, fishing, running, and music. He was named one of the 25 most influential people for conservation by *Outdoor Life* magazine, and…was named as Man of the Year by the American Sportfishing Association in 1997.

The former governor and his wife, Janet, live in
North Little Rock.[2]

Arkansas is the most lopsided Democratic state in the
USA. Eleven State Representatives were Republican when
Huckabee was elected in 1996, while there were eighty-nine
Democratic Representatives. The Senate was equally tipped
with four Republicans and thirty-one Democratic Senators.[3] To bring the state together in a bipartisan way and
be re-elected several times by huge percentages is nothing
short of a miracle, as well as a testimony of real leadership
with an anointed ability to shine among your constituents,
friends, and even foes.

While the governor of Massachusetts was raising fees,
about 700 million dollars, Huckabee cut taxes in Arkansas
ninety-four times. When Huckabee left office, he left it
with a surplus of almost 850 million dollars.[4] Huckabee
eliminated several taxes altogether and cut welfare by
almost 50 percent!

I quote Mike Huckabee here, from his book *Do the
Right Thing*: "We have to give voters a reason to choose us
as guardians of their future."[5]

four

PRESIDENT GEORGE W. BUSH

To: Mr. Tom Hudson, Thank you for your early commitment and dedication as a Charter Member of the campaign in Florida. Grassroots leaders like you are the key to building a winning team.

Best Wishes,

I BELIEVE HISTORY WILL be kind to our Cowboy President, once folks let it settle in how our mean, liberal media has taken over our country with their biased agenda! They really despised President Bush for being open about his Christian principles. They all aimed high, low, and at his heart to destroy him and his presidency. They did this to Mr. McCain and Sarah Palin as candidates as well. The liberal media will not be satisfied until they can officially announce to the world that we are in the days of Sodom and Gomorrah!

To refresh memories for some: when Bush took office, he inherited a declared recession and high unemployment figures. The enemy scheduled 9/11 to try to finish us off while we were down, but we were not out! By summer 2003, we had pulled out of the recession and were well on our way to achieving all of our economic dreams. We enjoyed unparalleled boom-time economic growth and prosperity through most of 2006.

I believe these four years—plus or minus—were the best in the history of this nation. People all over most of the country were getting new vehicles, four-wheelers, boats, vacation homes, new and bigger homes, and not many people even had to settle for a mobile home. Everyone was doing better than they had ever dreamed!

Wall Street got greedy, bankers and executives got more than greedy, and China finished their construction objectives in getting ready to show off to the world! They had taken years doing projects and preparing for the guests of the Olympics. Everyone who wanted a new home in America had purchased one, and the boom was over worldwide about the same time.

I know Mr. Bush made some mistakes; we are all human. But for the liberal media leading the individuals of this country to blame and bash Bush for all the bad that happened and is happening is prejudicial garbage. For people to actually believe it is scary! Remember that the last two years of Bush's presidency the Democrats were in control of

Congress. They had oversight of committee after committee. They were in charge and were responsible for steering us around problems. Maybe they fell asleep at the wheel! Also remember that this Democratic Congress' approval rating was much lower than that of President Bush.

The media has never given Bush credit for over four years of the best times in the history books. The Iraq War, losing lives, and the financial cost are terrible; however, there have been no attacks on our soil since 9/11. We are a safe country, and terrorists knew our cowboy would get them if they messed with us. According to Laura Bush, 50 million people were freed from tyranny because of Bush's actions.[1] His policies set a format to help the entire Middle East go toward democracy instead of tyranny. Real results can be counted from this war, which may be a first in history. My wish for the entire Bush family is for all of them to enjoy many happy years in the future!

I, for one, have had enough of the liberal media, and I turn them off. I have kicked them out of my home to stay. It's like kicking Satan out and locking the door. Please join with me. Let's protest the actions of the liberal media. With enough organization we could shut a lot of them down by not watching, not listening, and not buying their sponsors' products.

five

OPEN LETTER TO BLACK CONSERVATIVE CHRISTIANS

From My Heart to Yours

My son and grandson, Tim and Tyler. We welcome all races
to our annual Mt. Carmel Vacation Bible School. We worship
together as well as learn about Jesus and...ride the train.

F ELLOW CONSERVATIVE CHRISTIANS, I do not blame
you for being as loyal as possible to Barack Obama
the first time around. We should make every effort to
be loyal to our brethren and/or neighbor. *In business* that's
the way Christians should respond to each other. However,

in choosing our leaders, we need to let God's Holy Word and the Spirit of the Lord lead us.

My hope and prayer is that something I write personally to you in this letter or elsewhere in this book will, by the power of the Holy Spirit and the grace of God, allow you to see with an open mind and heart, as I have done my best to do in writing this book to determine my future party affiliation.

I wish I could talk to each one of you one on one!

In the Introduction of this book, I stated one of the reasons for writing it is that it might be utilized as a fact-finding exercise to help me in determining what political group I should affiliate with or change to. I know I needed to make a decision based on my beliefs and Christian principles, according to God's Word. I asked myself the questions, Where do I fit? Where can I do the most good for my country? Where do I need to serve to be loyal to my God and to best apply my ability based on my education and training? I want to be in the center of God's will.

Please consider with me the following, which is excerpted from Star Parker's column, "When Color Trumps Christianity."

> President Obama hosted a reception at the White House celebrating LGBT (Lesbian, Gay, Bisexual, Transgender) Pride month…Christians should take note and learn a few things about our…president…
>
> It tells us something that Mr. Obama had no time to host an event for the National Day of

Prayer. Nor did he have time to accept the invitation to convey greetings and a few remarks to the couple hundred thousand who came to Washington, as they do every January, for the March for Life. However, the LGBT Pride event did make it onto the president's busy schedule.

Here are parts of his remarks I think noteworthy for...Christians: First, we now know that Mr. Obama buys into reasoning equating the homosexual political movement to the black civil rights movement: "...it's not for me to tell you to be patient any more than it was for others to counsel patience to African Americans who were petitioning for equal rights a half century ago."

Second, Obama sees the black community as being a little slow on the uptake to grasp that homosexuality and same-sex marriage are okay. There still are those, according to him, "who don't yet fully embrace their gay brothers and sisters..." He deals with this, he said, by talking about it in front of "unlikely audiences," such as, "in front of African American church members"...

And, third, Obama talked about HIV/AIDS but didn't bother to mention that it's overwhelmingly blacks that this scourge is killing.

Why would our black president discuss HIV/AIDS and not mention that although blacks represent 12 percent of our population, they account for 50 percent of HIV/AIDS cases and half of HIV-related deaths? Or that the incidence of HIV/AIDS

infection per every 100,000 people is nine times
higher among blacks than whites?...

Apparently Obama considered this information irrel-
evant at the LGBT festivities. This would have been the
perfect opportunity to share these truths, but he opted out
because he did not care enough about his people.

Blacks, of course, made the difference in getting
Proposition 8 passed in California, which defined
marriage as between a man and a woman. They
then switched over and voted for Obama. Obama
has said he opposes same-sex marriage. Can this
really be so? He said at the White House event
that he's called for Congress to repeal the Defense
of Marriage Act. DOMA is the main obstacle to
nationalizing legalization of same-sex marriage. [If
he is successful with this, on top of so many other
things, we need to pray for the Rapture to come
quickly!]

Black Christians have a lot of soul searching
to do...But we also must retain clarity that these
many injustices were the result of race and color
trumping Christian principles. Particularly as sexu-
ally transmitted diseases kill our people, when a
third of all abortions are black babies, and the only
hope for future black prosperity is restoration of
the black family?[1]

All of this, along with much, much more, is an integral
part of the liberal Democratic Party's platform or agenda.
Most of them also despise our being a friend to Israel, along

with other un-Christian ideals. These are only a few of the things I looked at in deciding that the Democratic Party could almost be considered anti-God. As mentioned in this book's Introduction, this is why I'm embarrassed—as a Southern Baptist deacon and committed Christian—to have ever been registered as a Democrat!

I have analyzed, debated, prayed, fasted, and investigated, and I can't vote for anyone in this party! While neither Republicans nor their party are perfect, the Republican Party—which interestingly, was the party of Abraham Lincoln—is the party for me. They do uphold Christians and the principles we hold so dear.

It is my hope and prayer that each of you will consider these thoughts from my heart to yours.

We will never forget 9/11.

> Red, white, and blue will last forever. Somewhere between the red, white, and blue are me and you!
>
> John F. Kennedy, a Catholic liberal, had prepared a speech he never had the opportunity to give on that fateful night when he was assassinated. The speech was in response to the Supreme Court ruling to take prayer and Bibles out of our schools. Included in his prepared speech was Psalm 127:1, which says, "Unless the LORD builds the house, They labor in vain who build it; Unless the LORD guards the city, The watchman stays awake in vain."[2]

As I get older, I appreciate the Declaration of Independence more. This great document has led America toward a more perfect union for over 230 years. It has inspired people around the world!

> We hold these truths to be self-evident, that all men are created equal, that they are endowed by their Creator with certain unalienable Rights, that among these are Life, Liberty, and the pursuit of Happiness.[3]

This was only a dream in 1776, but by the grace of God, it has become reality for all of us in 2009. No matter how bleak the economy looks or how bad the jobless and foreclosure lists are, we are still part of the greatest country on the face of the earth in all of history.

Our rights come from our Creator, not from men or the government. Government belongs to "we the people" and exists only to secure the rights endowed by God to every citizen!

six

NEW ORLEANS

A small percentage of the mobile homes at the airport in Hope, Arkansas,
transported there from New Orleans

THE HURRICANE KATRINA aftermath in New
Orleans: the liberal media has used this as one
more reason to bash George Bush, FEMA, and the
federal government for "allowing" this storm to hit and for
everything that happened afterward!

My immediate reaction to the Katrina damage was to
rebuild New Orleans north and west of Lake Pontchar-
train. If that had happened, today you would have a
cleaned up New Orleans with surviving structures repaired
and spruced up and a north New Orleans that would have
space for safe future growth!

In Florida, we have state laws against building or rebuilding structures with floors below the one-hundred–year flood plain. If I had been president or the governor of Louisiana, this is the direction in which I would have lead. In Florida we may have had problems with ballots, but we follow excellent building codes!

At the very least, Governor Bobby Jindal could have done the right thing and built mobile home subdivisions on high ground north of the lake so that all the mobile homes President Bush provided could be placed. Instead, early on when it became difficult to find space to park them in the original New Orleans proper area, the governor apparently had FEMA deliver them approximately four hundred miles away from New Orleans. (These nice, furnished mobile homes were delivered to Hope, Arkansas!) I have seen this with my own eyes, and it is a sad sight to see, especially in view of the fact that even in November 2009, we still hear of displaced victims of Katrina who do not have homes to go back to. The shock of this still makes my wife and me sick to our stomachs. Just think of all these misplaced, probably hungry people without a shelter to call home and without hope!

Recently a lady called to invite me to a fundraising dinner to hear Governor Jindal speak. I told her that her invitation disgusted me, because from what I could see, he did not have the qualifications to be governor. Nonetheless, some people have even gone so far as to recommend him for a promotion to president due to the supposedly excellent job he has done for New Orleans and Louisiana. I'm sorry, but I was not impressed! I know the governor is a good man and has done many good things, but the things I have mentioned here are some of my pet peeves, I guess, from training in planning, building, and engineering.

These mobile homes I mentioned continue to take up hundreds of acres at the Hope, Arkansas, Airport, an old military base. Hypothetically, if there are two thousand units, this represents a cost of close to $4 million. I understand FEMA wants to sell them now for a few hundred dollars each, since they have begun to mold inside because of improper care!

I have seen some of these units going down the interstate, and they are marked "Scrap" in big, bold letters. They probably carry a title that FEMA also marked "For scrap only." This would prevent anyone from being able to get a permit to live in one of these units, even after spending thousands of dollars on cleaning and reconditioning.

I don't know a proper ending to this except to say, "Wow," or "Whoa! God have mercy on us!"

seven

SARAH PALIN, DOLLY PARTON, AND JIMMY CARTER

We are serious about our Dollywood annual parade.

GOVERNOR SARAH PALIN and Dolly Parton: I mention these together because they have quite a few similarities in backgrounds, raising, beliefs, and spunk. They have both been progressive and outstanding in their fields, and they are both entertaining!

My family and I had some fun a few years back with Dolly

Parton. We had purchased a retirement/vacation home near Pigeon Forge, Tennessee, and Dolly was having her annual parade through town to open Dollywood for the 1999 season. My sister-in-law, Linda, was chauffeuring us in her white Caddy. To get to know Dolly better during the parade as it moved north in the northbound lanes of the parkway, we followed her during the parade, getting out of the car at each intersection to wave and speak to Dolly. As soon as she would pass through one intersection, we would jump back in the Caddy and rush ahead to the next intersection. There, we would again jump out of the car and run to the street curb, awaiting Dolly's arrival so that we could repeat our very enthusiastic appreciation (hollering to the top of our lungs, waving furiously, and blowing the horn on the white Caddy) to get her attention. We did this through several intersections, and at about the third intersection, Dolly began to recognize us and seemed quite amused with our enthusiasm. Those Kerce sisters sure do enjoy fun times together, and my nephew, Daniel, and I enjoyed it with them.

As an ordained deacon and an active member of a Southern Baptist Church, I have been doing mission work for years. During the past five years, I have visited Mexico several times and helped organize a new church in a village within Cozumel. In this work I have traveled in at least twenty-five states, nineteen again during the past nineteen months. I have worked the longest, nearly a week, in Alaska and in Arkansas because of conditions in these two states. I was able to do a lot of comparison in the populations, roads, bridges, etc., and I discovered that Alaska should be a fairly easy state to govern because of such small numbers in the aforementioned areas. Also, the revenue from oil is a beautiful deal for the state and its officials, and the population even shares the wealth!

My wife and I like Sarah Palin very much and voted for her for vice president, feeling she was qualified for the job. She brought enthusiasm to the Republican Party and did it with class and distinction. I hope she will become the U.S. Senator from Alaska someday and not run for president, because the liberal media would have a sausage grinding over that.

Being president of the USA has become perilous. A lady governor or senator could possibly get by the liberal news media. The same holds true for the lady governor's husband. However, he could not get away with protecting his wife on the national and international stage. The liberal media will not change, and it would be devastating for her, her family, and the United States!

I, along with many others, believe McCain could have been elected president if he had chosen Huckabee for vice president! Here's what happened: the Independents are a strong group of independent thinkers. They represent approximately thirty percent of the actual voters, and they strongly impact presidential elections.[1] Many Independents were leaning for McCain until the Wall Street meltdown occurred in September 2008. This group shifted at this happening about three weeks before the election because of McCain's age and fear that Sarah could not handle the president's job if McCain passed away. Once they made up their minds, nothing could have changed it in these complex times we are in now.

No one except Palin knows what she is up to. Now she has resigned as governor. My biggest fear is that if she were to get on the Republican ticket for 2012, the Independents, who will decide the election again, will not go for a ticket with her on it. Also, it has come to my attention that although I admire Palin and think a lot of her, if she seeks the Republican nomination, in all probability she would split the vote so badly that the true conservative, electable, qualified candidate probably would not be the nominee. To me and America that would be devastating. Plus, the prejudiced, liberal news media would be fighting her all the way. They are not going to let up!

Because of his lack of experience it seems to some like Obama is letting Reid, Pelosi, his numerous advisors, and their lobbyists run the country. All he seemingly has to do is wear the hat, travel, and read the teleprompter to find out their decisions for the country. This is how you unite the Democratic Congress: you do what they tell you and don't worry about your promises, your word, or your vision. Just run with your crowd, right or wrong. How sad for America!

Here is what Mike Huckabee has to say about Nancy Pelosi:

> Here's a story about a lady named Nancy
> A ruthless politician, but dressed very fancy
> Very ambitious, she got herself elected Speaker
> But as for keeping secrets, she proved quite a "leaker."
>
> She flies on government planes coast to coast
> And doesn't mind that our economy is toast
> She makes the Air Force squire her in the military jets
> There's room for her family, her staff, and even her pets.
>
> Until now she annoyed us, but her gaffes were mostly funny;
> Even though it was painful to watch her waste our tax money.
> But now her wacky comments are no laughing matter;
> She's either unwilling to tell the truth, or she's mad as a hatter!
>
> She sat in briefings and knew about enhanced interrogation;
> But claims she wasn't there, and can't give an explanation.

She disparages the CIA and says they are a bunch
    of liars;
Even the press aren't buying it and they're stoking
    their fires.
I think Speaker Pelosi has done too much
    speaking;
And instead of her trashing our intelligence
    officials, it's her nose that needs tweaking.

If forced to believe whether the CIA and her
    colleagues in Congress are lying;
Or it's Speaker Pelosi whose credibility and career
    is dying.
I believe in the integrity of the men and woman
    who sacrifice to keep us safe;
Not the woman who has been caught flat-footed,
    lying to our face.

I say it here and I say it rather clear—
It's time for Nancy Pelosi to resign and get out of
    here.[2]

Now, Jimmy Carter—I remember the excitement of
his election to the presidency! He was apparently a good
governor of Georgia. Some of the excitement was because
he was from Georgia and was known to be a bright Christian, a Sunday school teacher, businessman, and farmer. I
was disappointed because all I remember about his faith
was that he said he was born again. I do not remember
him doing anything to help the teachers, businessmen, or
the farmers. He definitely could not manage the economy,
as inflation spiraled the worst in his term that I can ever

remember. Home sales stopped cold, and values dropped. Interest rates soared to nearly 20 percent.

I do remember the excitement of almost personally seeing President Carter play softball! My wife and I had just taken our young family on vacation to Pigeon Forge, Tennessee. On the way back, in the middle of Atlanta, we decided we had the time to go 120 miles out of our way to see the sights in and around Plains, Georgia, since our president was from that area. Other than the peanut fields and support warehouses, etc., we were impressed with seeing the Plains community enjoying a spirited Sunday afternoon softball game. By the time we arrived, going by the game, we were exhausted and anxious to get our young family home to Lake City, Florida. So I put the pedal to the metal and brought my family on home.

After unloading the van and settling down to rest, somebody turned the TV on to the news. We could not believe our ears when we realized the newsman was talking about the softball game we passed in Plains, Georgia. We had been to Plains on the right day and the right hour to see President Jimmy Carter pitch the game but drove right by it!

During his presidency, his team played the press core regularly. We are still disappointed to this day. My biggest disappointment in him is he is still getting in the country's business all over the world today. He has so many weird views that coincide with Obama's, particularly the disdain they openly show for Israel, God's chosen country and people. I will not delve too far into this except to recommend a five hundred page book about Jimmy Carter if you want to read the details for yourself. *Jimmy Carter: The*

Liberal Left and World Chaos is written by Dr. Mike Evans and is very thorough and informative. Remember, my book is for a different purpose and intent. Here are some excerpts from Mike Evans's book:

> It was Jimmy Carter who modeled for Barack Obama the intricate steps to the political "flip-flop hip-hop"—the mating dance of an aspiring liberal left president.
>
> The presidential election was a public sounding board for the much touted failures of the Republican Party.
>
> He ran against a disgraced president and his policies; he ran in the aftermath of an unpopular war on a platform of 'human rights;' and he won.
>
> His theme was "change" and that is what America and the world got.
>
> He kept his word and change began.
>
> No, not Barack Obama, Jimmy Carter![3]

Well, readers, it looks to me like Obama is following a blueprint, the world Carter built or tore apart.

eight

TEA PARTIES

A s Tea Party Day approached, the Office of Homeland Security issued a report warning of "right wing
extremist" gatherings. Can anyone doubt the intent
of this report? Now is the time for all patriotic Americans to
band together and expose the unpatriotic "big spenders."

The following is from an article written by Judith Lowrey
and published in the *Lake City Reporter*:

DID T.E.A. PARTY ACHIEVE GOAL?

With the National T.E.A. Party Day event of April
15 over, the question begs to be asked, "Did we, as
organizers, supporters, American citizens, patriots,
liberals, conservatives, Democrats (and yes there
were several in attendance), Republicans, Libertar-
ians or just plain old bystanders have the right to
be there, or were we just the whining complainers
speaking to the disgruntled citizens?"

Here are my thoughts. The right to assemble
allows people to gather for peaceful and lawful
purposes. Implicit within this right is the right to
association and belief. Freedom of assembly, sometimes used interchangeably with the freedom of
association, is the individual right to come together
with other individuals and collectively express,
promote, pursue and defend common interests.
The right to freedom of association is recognized
as a human right, a political freedom and a civil
liberty. Now, with all that being said, let me give
you an idea of what the National T.E.A. Party is
about. T.E.A. is an acronym for Taxed Enough
Already. It is not about left or right, Democrats or
Republicans. It is not about who is President. It is
about taxes! No more, no less! I am a conservative
Christian. Up until recently, I only exercised my
political opinion with my vote. Yes, I am Republican and I felt that my party did not represent me

adequately. I also believe that this is not a political issue, it is an American issue.

While not my choice, the president of the United States of America deserves respect for the position that he holds.

The theme for the Lake City T.E.A. Party was one of bi-partisanship. I did not discourage "freedom of speech," yet I, as one of the organizers, made it clear that this event was about the over-taxation and over-the-top spending of our tax dollars by all elected officials, not who is president. I discouraged any political signage that pointed negatively to any individual.

This event was about taxation and the reckless spending of hard-earned American tax payers' dollars by all elected officials, no matter the political affiliation.

The T.E.A. Parties nationwide were peaceful events, with an occasional "main-stream reporter" expressing their opinion, rather than just reporting the news, causing occasional disruption and discord!

The National T.E.A. Party will continue on a national and local level. Additional events will be organized, whether by me or some other concerned American Citizen.

The 9-12 Project will continue to gather and support local citizens who believe in America and its ideals—Americans who desire to retain what our founding fathers have provided for us and for what countless Americans have died: The right to live free.

The concept of, "We surround them" will not go away. It is time that all people of America stand up and let their voices be heard. I am Taxed Enough Already! I am concerned, as a nation, that my hard-earned tax dollars are being spent in a manner that is not good for America or her citizens.

I am concerned that we, as a people, are not being heard. I am not a right-wing extremist carrying political propaganda (the U.S. Constitution). I am an American.

If you are interested in being a part of this active movement by concerned North Florida residents and you are not happy with the direction that our government is taking with your hard-earned tax dollars, please visit www.the912project.com. It starts at home!

Thank you for this opportunity to speak uncensored!

—JUDITH LOWREY[1]
LAKE CITY TEA PARTY ORGANIZER

My being led to write this book in the early morning hours of April 15, 2009, had nothing to do with April 15, Tax Day and Tea Party Day.

The following is a short list of comments about Tea Parties in the press:

Over at…MSNBC, the jokes about tea parties have been lewd and crude. Some commentators think such protests are just stupid…

So it seemed a kind of truth-seeking mission to visit Denver's Tax Day demonstration, a gathering of men and women whose ideas were pretty well summed up in the posters they were carrying.

"Haste, waste and fear is not a plan," said one. "200 years to build a nation, one election to destroy it," said another…Anyone still suspecting President Barack Obama was the day's hero need only have glanced at this message: "Hail to the thief."[2]

The number of Tea Parties held across the country and the number of people who attended is staggering. The whole Tea Party phenomenon was patterned after the 1773 Boston Tea Party and was intended to be a signal to Washington that the spending spree coming on top of an already huge debt could be economically devastating. If not stopped, this will bankrupt the future of our children and grandchildren.

nine

OBAMA'S PRAISE FOR TIM TEBOW AND THE GATORS

Headed to the game

I READ AN ARTICLE titled "Obama Praises Tebow, Gators" by Bill Theobald that struck me as interesting. Here are excerpts from that article:

Finally someone was able to stop the University of Florida Football Team.

President Obama was able to keep the speedy Gators in one place for about an hour Thursday during a White House ceremony to honor the team for last season's national title.

"There is something about Coach (Urban) Meyer's Team. They just have a lot of heart," Obama said in the East Room of the White House with team members and coaches behind him. "That's a reflection of coaching values that talk about character and integrity and not just winning."[1]

Yes, President Obama, I'm encouraged that "yes, you can" see this in the Florida Gator coach and his team. I just yearn for a president and leader of our free world who can not only see this but make this a part of his own personal life, a president who can really know about coaching values, who can talk about integrity and not just winning!

It takes a special person who is saved by God and anointed by his or her Savior to lead by example. I know such a person, and I learned from him as he was a candidate for president last year. I have grown to love and respect him very much. Huckabee believes there really is not a lot wrong with the good ole' USA or its people, and there's probably not a whole lot of change needed; we just need better coaching.

Theobald's article continues:

The president heaped special praise on star quarterback, Tim Tebow: "Heisman Trophy winner—that's what I'm talking about."

"Tim's an inspiration to so many," Obama said. "A guy whose true strength comes not from the gym but from his faith."[2]

Mr. President, I'm so thankful you can see this in others like our quarterback, Tim Tebow! It gives me hope that we will have a president one day that will lead our Congress, this nation, and the free world the way Tim leads the Gators and others around him.

Back in September 2008, I sent you and most of Congress a challenge by U.S. mail, a verse that includes a prescription for correcting the problems of this country. It should have been received just as the Wall Street bailout talks began. We could have saved trillions of dollars if this prescription had taken or ever does take hold of Congress.

If my people, who are called by my name, will humble themselves and pray and seek my face and turn from their wicked ways, then will I hear from heaven and will forgive their sin and will heal their land.

—2 Chronicles 7:14

ten

THE IRAQ WAR

My favorite barn in Tennessee

I HOPE NEW YORK commentator Deroy Murdock doesn't mind me sharing some of his commentary about this to those who read my book. Mr. Murdock is a media fellow with the Hoover Institution on War, Revolution, and Peace at Stanford University. He is also a columnist with the Scripps Howard News Service. His story goes a long way toward setting the record straight for all time. He wrote this column as if George Bush were addressing these truths to the nation.

What this country needs now is more truths revealed so that we will know how to go forward and sort out whom and what to believe. Between the liberal news media, their prejudiced reporting, and overzealous politicians saying different things to different groups—making different promises—and then doing what Congress tells them to do, we have gotten into a mess. Congress does what lobbyists and pollsters, who seem to poll only the liberals with their party, tell them to do.

THE DEMOCRATS' WAR
BY DEROY MURDOCK

In the next few weeks, President Bush should deliver a speech along these lines:

My fellow Americans:

March 2007 marks the fourth anniversary of the U.S.-led liberation of Iraq. Operation Iraqi Freedom's final outcome remains a mystery. But despite the chaos on TV every evening, and the challenges that emerge every morning, this effort has yielded plenty of good. America and its allies deposed a bloodthirsty despot who dispatched 300,000 of his constituents to mass graves. Saddam Hussein now occupies his own grave and no longer threatens his countrymen and neighbors…

I also want to thank several brave Democrats who helped get us here today.

"Saddam Hussein is a tyrant who has tortured and killed his own people, even his own family members, to maintain his iron grip on power," Senator Hillary Rodham Clinton said…in October 2002. "He used chemical weapons on Iraq Kurds and on Iranians, killing over 20,000 people."

"Hussein," Clinton added, "has also given aid, comfort, and sanctuary to terrorists, including al Qaeda members."

Clinton was correct. Saddam Hussein sprayed poison gas on his own people and sprayed cash on terrorists from the West Bank to West Street. After al Qaeda's February 1993 bombing of Manhattan's World Trade Center, Saddam Hussein gave Iraqi Abdul Rahman Yasin a house and a stipend in Baghdad. Yasin built the bomb that rocked the Twin Towers…

Clinton was absolutely right in 2002. I thank her for her leadership and for giving me the authority to unseat this butcher.

"It would be naïve to the point of grave danger not to believe that, left to his own devices, Saddam Hussein will provoke, misjudge, or stumble into a future, more dangerous confrontation with the civilized world."

Senator John Kerry was justified in saying this… Senator Kerry was astute to recognize this danger, and I thank him for empowering me to neutralize this global menace.

As then-Senator John Edwards said…Hussein had "violated the cease-fire agreement. The reality is that we can't allow him to continue on this same track. And I also believe that we can't be secure, and the region can't be secure, as long as he's still in power."

Senator Edwards was on the money…

I thank Senator Edwards for his wisdom, and for his vote to unplug the thug.

These three, along with 26 other Senate Democrats, joined 82 House Democrats to authorize this conflict. Unreliable as pre-war intelligence may have been regarding the scope of Hussein's WMDs, these 111 Democrats accepted the analyses that I honestly and sincerely shared with them. In March 2005, the Silverman/Robb Commission said it "found no evidence of 'politicization' of the intelligence community's assessments concerning Iraq's reported WMD programs."

Let me thank these three Democrats, and the others who voted to remove Saddam Hussein, for their courage and support as America decided to liberate Iraq. What happens next over there is unclear. What we do know is that America's mission in Iraq is not just my war—it's their war, too.[1]

If we can ever get a semblance of truth for the public to believe about the past and present, it would hopefully restore some integrity in government. And, integrity would help restore the confidence, faith, and hope of the people as well!

The voting percentages may even go up if "we the people" had any confidence in the media and our elected officials. This is all going to have to take place before forgiveness can, and forgiveness is going to have to take place before God will hear our prayers and restore this nation.

eleven

FAIR TAX

When you purchase your new boat, your federal income tax is paid at the same time. You do not pay it again and again...only at the point of purchase!

B E CAUTIOUS WHEN you hear the terms *flat tax* and *fair tax* utilized, or you may fall into the same logical assumption I've had the past year or so. I thought they were one and the same or at least similar. Not so. The only similarities are that they both start with *F* and have four letters.

From my understanding, the flat tax would *not* be much better than the conglomeration we have now!

If you want a thorough understanding of the fair tax, you need to get *The Fair Tax Book*, written by Neal Boortz and Congressman John Linder. Also Mike Huckabee's best-selling book *Do the Right Thing* has a great chapter on the fair tax.

The first good thing the fair tax would do is to eliminate the IRS. The fair tax would shift taxes from being on what we earn to on the things we buy. (It would be a consumption tax on most of our purchases, similar to our state sales tax.) Therefore, if the IRS still had a duty, it would basically be as a receiving or collection agency. They would receive the money from retailers where we all buy our products.

I guess your first question would be like mine, would the state sales tax continue? Yes, I assume it would, but the additional tax you would pay at the register would be in place of your income tax, which is one of the many advantages of the fair tax. You would only pay taxes when you buy things.

No one would have to fill out forms. It would encourage everyone to work all they could and not be penalized for their hard work, longer hours, initiative, or production. It would also encourage selling for a profit and entrepreneurship.

The authors of the fair tax estimate that the people in the top one-third income bracket would benefit by an average of four and one-half percent under the fair tax. Those in the middle would benefit by seven and one-half percent, and those in the bottom one-third income bracket could benefit by as much as twelve percent. If I understand this correctly, you could look at these percentages as that much more money in your pocket. It would be like a pay raise, so to speak!

The authors of the fair tax estimate that additional economic benefits would occur.

- Gross domestic product would increase by 10.5 percent.
- Capitol stock would increase by 42 percent.
- Labor supply would increase by 4 percent.
- Output would increase by 12 percent.
- Real wages would increase by 8 percent.[1]

One of the things that make it tough for us entrepreneurs and small business owners to survive is the cost of compliance with the complicated tax laws. It is estimated that Americans spend more than $250 billion a year complying with the complicated IRS tax code.[2] (Can you imagine what we could enjoy with this kind of saving?)

The fair tax benefits everyone: singles, married, divorced, and any other status. No one, individually or collectively, is penalized, nor are corporations. It is also believed that the fair tax would give our American economy a significant boost, which it so desperately needs right now.

In closing, here's something I had not thought about until a truck driver in Michigan named Randy Bishop came up with it: the fair tax would even collect money for the treasury from illegal workers and visitors to America, along with many others who do not share in this now![3]

twelve

FREEDOM OF CHOICE ACT

They are all precious in His sight.

THE AMERICAN CENTER for Law and Justice (ACLJ) has created a petition against the Freedom of Choice Act that will be sent to our representatives and United States senators. I gladly took part in these petitions as well as gave a contribution to help defray costs! The petition states:

A majority of Americans clearly abhor the practice of partial-birth abortion. Congress passed a federal ban against it, the President signed the ban, and the Supreme Court of the United States has now upheld the ban.

It was inappropriate for members of Congress to introduce the "Freedom of Choice" Act, which would totally reverse the decision of the people, the Congress, the President, and the Supreme Court.

To replace a ban on partial-birth abortion with a ban on federal regulation of abortion would represent an outrageous affront to the American people.

It is also of dubious constitutionality to make this bill retroactive.

We urge you to use your influence with the Committee to kill this bill rather than sending it to the floor for a vote.[1]

The following is my paraphrase of a letter Jay Alan Sekulow, chief counsel of the ACLJ, sent to concerned citizens. I have included this so you will have firsthand knowledge of what is going on right now in Washington concerning the abortion issue.

Dear Friend,

If you had no opinion about abortion—if it were a "shrug of the shoulders" issue for you—then you wouldn't care about what's happening in Washington today. But because you care about the lives of unborn babies, you need to be aware: Abortion is roaring back.

President Barack Obama, newly sworn in, made it clear as a candidate what he'd do in his coming term: "The first thing I'd do as President is sign the Freedom of Choice Act. That's the first thing that I'd do." But this anticipated legislation would *roll back the federal ban on partial-birth abortion*—as well as other major pro-life legislation.

Parents have to be notified? Not under Freedom of Choice.

Federal limits on abortion funding? Not under Freedom of Choice.

Roe v Wade? Freedom of Choice would virtually enshrine it into federal law.

Estimates indicate that as many as 125,000 more babies will be killed every year under this so-called "Freedom of Choice."

Let me tell you why I'm giving you this information. My name is Jay Alan Sekulow, and I serve as Chief Counsel for the American Center for Law and Justice (ACLJ)—an organization dedicated to preserving life and liberty in this country and strategic parts of the world.

For more than fifteen years, we have worked to protect the unborn and uphold the sanctity of life, as well as preserve religious liberties for citizens all across this nation.

We've been involved at every level of American life—from local school boards all the way up to the Supreme Court of the United States, where I have argued twelve cases.

By God's grace, the ACLJ is perfectly positioned, from our offices across the street from the Supreme Court and down the street from Congress, to lead the fight effectively for the sake of the unborn.

And today, the lives of unborn babies are on the line. With this new President, and even more pro-abortion Members of Congress, we are at risk of the Freedom of Choice Act moving very, very quickly to a vote.

Yes, it would be an incredibly brazen move by our newly elected national leaders to pass and sign such a bill into law.

It would basically be a slap in the face for pro-life America—especially since surveys indicate clearly that a majority want restrictions, if not an outright ban, on abortion in this country.

It's astonishing to consider that such a thing could happen. Such a power play by our new leaders could completely decimate the fight against abortion in our nation.

On behalf of caring people like you, we fought for the ban on partial-birth abortion, and saw it passed by Congress and signed by the President as an expression of the will of the people. We also filed briefs and worked in defense of the constitutionality of the ban all the way to the Supreme Court of the United States.

It's almost numbing to think of the torture-killing of babies as they're being born suddenly being legal again. And for this tragedy to occur under the banner of something as innocuous-sounding as "freedom of choice"—frankly, it's sickening.

thirteen

LET'S HELP THE JEWS GET HOME

Some "folks" at a book signing

THE FOLLOWING IS from a fundraising letter I received from the On Wings of Eagles organization.

We have seen the pattern before. When a nation's economy is in shambles and people are without the bare necessities of life (e.g., food, water) they desperately cry out for a cause and someone to blame!

In Germany under the Nazis, this pattern led to the Holocaust with the slaughter of over six million innocent people. Mothers, fathers, and children were incinerated in ovens running around the clock.

Today this pattern is happening in Europe, the Middle East, South America, and other locations. It's fueled by radical Islamists, Communists, extreme nationalists, neo-Nazis, and other groups driven by their hatred for Israel, Jews, and the West.

Ultranationalist leaders in Russia and other countries continue to accuse Jews of starting World War II and provoking the Holocaust.

In Istanbul, Turkey, a car bomb destroyed two synagogues, killing twenty-three people.

In Argentina, in the suburbs of Paris, and in the countries of the former Soviet Union, Synagogues, Community Centers, and other places where Jews gather are targets for destruction.

The former Soviet Union has the third-largest Jewish population in the world behind the United States and Israel.

There is growing threat of radical Islamists in the former Soviet Republic dominated by Muslims.

There is an urgent need for help to rescue these people!

In Ezekiel 39:28 God said, "Then they will know that I am the LORD their God, for though I sent them into exile among the nations, I will gather them to their own land, not leaving any behind."

> On Wings of Eagles, an outreach of the International Fellowship of Christians and Jews, has already provided rescue airlifts for more than two hundred thousand Jewish immigrants, helping "gather them to their own land," to Israel.
>
> Once they reach Israel, On Wings of Eagles provides support, helps them find housing, learn the language, and enter the culture of Israel.
>
> …This is God's chosen people, they are refugees, not tourists, leaving with only the clothes on their backs and a few bags in their hands!

I included this in my book because on April 15, 2009, the instruction that I gleaned from the Holy Spirit was to put in this book things I saw, heard, and sensed until there was a valuable book of resources and wisdom for the people of the USA. It is my prayer that some will be lead to support On Wings of Eagles.

In a recent update posted by Dr. Mike Evans, he explained that Barack Obama continues with his attitude toward Israel and the Gaza Strip, which is really the Holy Land area, as do Clinton, Carter, Biden, and many others. They want to just give this area to the Palestinian terrorists and thugs. Obama has ordered Israel to stop construction in the Gaza area. But they will not settle for just this area; they want it all. He continued (my paraphrase):

> Satan wants this Gaza area too! He wants to make a garbage dump out of Mount Calvary, where Jesus died for our sins, and of the Garden Tomb and the Via Dolorosa.

The devil wants to wipe out every tangible witness from the earth that Jesus was crucified and rose from the dead in resurrection power! The devil wants Islam to have its way. Satan knows the prophecy in Luke 21:24, that Jerusalem will be in the hands of the Jews when our Lord returns. This is Satan's greatest fear!

I wonder if it would be legal for believers to contribute funds and form a militia to help this area be defended.

The following is an article written by Star Parker that was published in a local newspaper. It provides some excellent insight.

OBAMA FOREIGN POLICY SHOWS CHANGE IN VALUES
BY STAR PARKER

Barack Obama's obvious comfort level with leaders of un-free countries shouldn't surprise anyone. He is not only our first black president. He is also our first president who doesn't like the free country he was elected to lead and feels his job is to change it.

Obama's cordial encounter with Venezuelan thug Hugo Chavez, his bow of deference in London to the Saudi Arabian king, are extensions of behavior we have always seen on the black left. Jesse Jackson openly embraced Chavez, as well as having maintained relations with the likes of Libyan dictator Muammar Qaddafi and Yasir Arafat.

This should be kept in mind as our president now makes his own effort to bring peace to the Middle East.

It should be clear to anyone conscious and watching that central to Obama's Middle East strategy is to disabuse the long held notion that there exists a "special relationship" between the United States and Israel. The sense of unique kinship between our country and the Jewish state has existed since Israel's founding just 60 years ago.

The Arab world has always resented the US–Israel connection and has felt that because of this, Americans would never be an honest broker in Arab-Israeli negotiations.

Obama is out to change this. His first eleven months in office, from his very first television interview—given to an Arab television network—have focused on warming up our relations with Islamic nations and cooling down our Israeli ones.

We should appreciate that this shift is more than a technical change in diplomatic strategy. It reflects a change in values.

The "special" American-Israeli relationship has always reflected the shared values and traditions of the two countries. A commitment to freedom sustained by traditional Judeo-Christian core values…

The great American writer Mark Twain visited the Holy Land in 1867 before Jews made their miraculous return to their ancient homeland. He reported that there was nothing there. "Palestine is desolate and unlovely."

You have to be either blind or have a political agenda to refuse to see the incredible miracle that has occurred in the rebirth of the Jewish nation.

Of course, there is a special relationship between the United States and Israel. The same values and traditions have produced in both places freedom and prosperity from nothing.

Should we denigrate Arabs and Muslims? Certainly not. But anyone who thinks that peace and prosperity will come from abandoning those very values that got us to where we are, and along with this our friends who share those values, is deeply misguided.

Unfortunately, today we have an American president who is set on doing just that. Principled Americans and Israelis should tighten seatbelts and prepare to defend the truths we hold dear.[1]

Remember this extreme metamorphic state or condition of our country that I am writing about seemed to begin during Bill Clinton's campaign for the presidency in 1992. From information I'm receiving from books and other sources, it will probably continue until sometime in 2013 or thereabouts. Future predictions I will write about later come from experts' opinions.

THE ANT AND THE GRASSHOPPER

This one is a little different: two different versions [of the same story], two different morals.

Old Version

The ant works hard in the withering heat all summer long, building his house and laying up supplies for the winter. The grasshopper thinks the ant is a fool and laughs and dances and plays the summer away. Come winter, the ant is warm and well fed. The grasshopper has no food or shelter, so he dies out in the cold.

Moral of the story: Be responsible for yourself!

Modern Version

The ant works hard in the withering heat and the rain all summer long building his house and laying up supplies for the winter. The grasshopper thinks the ant is a fool and laughs and dances and plays the summer away. Come winter, the shivering grasshopper calls a press conference and demands to know why the ant should be allowed to be warm and well fed while he is cold and starving.

CBS, NBC, PBS, CNN, and ABC show up to provide pictures of the shivering grasshopper next to a video of the ant in his comfortable home with a table filled with food. America is stunned by the sharp contrast.

How can this be, that in a country of such wealth, this poor grasshopper is allowed to suffer so? Kermit the Frog appears on Oprah with the grasshopper and everybody cries when they sing, "It's Not Easy Being Green."

ACORN stages a demonstration in front of the ant's house where the news stations film the group singing, "We shall overcome." Then Rev. Jeremiah Wright has the group kneel down to pray to God for the grasshopper's sake. President Obama condemns the ant and blames President Bush, President Reagan, Christopher Columbus, and the Pope for the grasshopper's plight.

Nancy Pelosi and Harry Reid exclaim in an interview with Larry King that the ant has gotten rich off the back of the grasshopper, and both call for an immediate tax hike on the ant to make him pay his fair share. Finally, the EEOC drafts the Economic Equity & Anti-Ant Act retroactive to the beginning of the summer.

The ant is fined for failing to hire a proportionate number of green bugs and, having nothing left to pay his retroactive taxes, his home is confiscated by the Government Green Czar and given to the grasshopper.

The story ends as we see the grasshopper and his free-loading friends finishing up the last bits of the ant's food while the government house he is in, which as you recall, just happens to be the ant's old house, crumbles around them because the grasshopper doesn't maintain it.

The ant has disappeared in the snow, never to be seen again. The grasshopper is found dead in a drug related incident, and the house, now abandoned, is taken over by a gang of spiders who terrorize the ramshackle, once prosperous, and once peaceful neighborhood. The entire Nation collapses bringing the rest of the free world with it.

Moral of the story: Be careful how you vote in 2010 [and future elections].[2]

fourteen

THE COMING OF A NEW
WORLD ORDER

I F YOU WANT a thorough understanding of our economic system and what is going on, you need to purchase *The New Economic Disorder* by Dr. Larry Bates, published by Excel Books. Dr. Bates seems to have the best under-standing of anyone accessible to us.

He is highly qualified. He was a member of the Tennessee House of Representatives and is a former bank CEO. He is an economist and has his own radio show. He is CEO of Information Radio Network and IRN USA Radio News.

While in the Tennessee Legislature, he was Chairman of its Committee on Banking and Commerce. He has also taught in the state college system and the Bank Administrative Institute.

He writes:

> Today in America we are living in a fool's paradise...The money manipulators have successfully created the illusion of prosperity through the most massive creation of debt and paper money that has ever occurred in history...And that's just the tip of the iceberg about to ram us!...
>
> One thing will decide whether you'll be one of the winners or one of the losers—knowledge. John 8:32 says, "And ye shall know the truth, and the truth shall make you free."
>
> ...the term *new world order* is merely code for "one world socialism," with an elite ruling class to govern the rest of us under their demonic system.
>
> The elements and phrases of this new world order...are (1) the new economic order...(2) the new political order, and (3) the new religious order. It is my belief that the mechanism that has been set up to manage us all is a world government, an antichrist system, headquartered at the United Nations.
>
> Years ago, several of our editorial staff and I visited the headquarters of the United Nations in New York City, or as the world bureaucrats call it, "the sovereign territory of the world." When we

entered the U.N. complex, we were reminded at the gate that we were leaving the territory of the United States and were now entering world soil...

As we entered the main complex of the U.N. headquarters, we could see the meditation room off to our right. Also in this area is a very prominent wall-sized, stained-glass mural depicting all of the religions of the world coming together into one. In the upper left-hand corner of this mural is an image of Jesus Christ. However, in the very center of the mural is a large serpent. As our group walked down a darkened corridor toward the meditation room, we observed a large stone altar on which a meditation light was shining. Placed in front of the altar were eleven chairs, which I believe symbolically represent what we read in Daniel 7:24: "...out of this kingdom are ten kin."[1]

Dr. Bates continues:

The new world order is nothing new, and it's not going to be orderly...

The proponents...give lip service to the ideas of free enterprise and free markets...The pinnacle for such plans is to bring all people and nations of the world under a one-world government. That one world government includes a one world economic system we call "the new economic order."[2]

This is only phase one of their plan for the whole world, in which *things are very ripe for this to usher in soon!*

...the "Human Development Report," a report released by the Social and Economic Council of the United Nations in June of 1994, says: "A world central bank is essential for the twenty-first century for sound macro-economic management for global financial stability and for assisting the economic expansion of the poor nations."

They go on to say: "It will take some time and probably some international financial crisis before a full-scale world central bank can be created."[3]

June 1994 to September 2008 equals fourteen years and two months—that is some time!

Needless to say, one could get the idea they are tired of waiting. Time is money! I personally had a very uneasy feeling about the Wall Street jitterbug and the whole bank bailout mess, wondering from day one if it was a set-up to force the results of the election and other things. "The swaps" Senator Byron Dorgan expressed his fear of were done in 1994 also.

I won't even comment on how this ties into chapters 14, 15, and 16 in this book. I will let each reader digest it for him or herself.

fifteen

THE SENATOR WHO SAW IT COMING

My youngest grandson and I were checking out this rig!

THE ARTICLE THAT follows is an excerpt from "The Senator Who Saw It Coming," by Eric Adelson. It was published in *Newsweek*'s April 13, 2009, issue.

Future historians rummaging through the archives of the *Washington Monthly* might stumble upon a chilling article about a coming "financial conflagration… [E]very taxpayer in the country is on the line." The author was not some alarmist wacko, but a U.S. senator. And the year was not 2007, or even 2001. North Dakota Sen. Byron Dorgan expressed his fear of "exotic new derivatives called 'swaps'" way back in 1994. Five years later, when Congress passed legislation lowering the barriers between brokerages and banks, Dorgan told *The New York Times*, "I think we will look back in 10 years' time and say we should not have done this." It's been 10 years, and Dorgan was dead-on. He spoke to Eric Adelson while visiting flood victims in his home state.

How did you see this coming?

I saw the development of these complicated financial instruments…and it occurred to me that it's an unbelievable amount of risk. I introduced several pieces of legislation to regulate it, but my warnings were widely ignored.

Why?

I guess they thought I was old-fashioned. The financial establishment had no interest in slowing down the march toward modernization. But the firewalls were made of tissue paper.

What was it like watching your fears realized?

It makes you sick. I felt strongly that if the banks want to gamble, go to Las Vegas. There's very little solace in being right, given the carnage. This is one of the most expensive lessons in American history.

What are you calling for now?

There needs to be a select committee of the U.S. Senate. We need to know what has happened here. I don't think anyone has established a narrative. We also need to restore a portion of the separation [between the banks and the brokers]. The securitization of credit has to be dramatically changed or abolished.

How are these ideas being received?

I requested a meeting with the president last week, and I put together a group of six other senators to join me. We presented him with what we thought was necessary financial reform.

And?

I remain worried that modernization can't put a patch on things. There's a culture that's been developed on Wall Street and in Washington that what was done was a worthwhile thing because we were competing. We all want healthy banks. That's important. But what has happened is the big companies have spun out of control, like hogs in a corn crib.

One of the proponents of the change in regulations was then Treasury secretary Lawrence Summers, who's now Obama's Director of Economic Council. How confident are you that real reform can happen with Summers by the president's side?

[*Pause*] I offered the president my advice about financial advisers early on. I'll leave it at that.[1]

Readers, I urge you to please read and reread this story's last paragraph. It appears that Senator Byron Dorgan has done all he can for our country. I wonder how many other Congressmen and women have run into roadblocks like this. They are the patriotic ones that do not want to see our country's economy collapse. They put their necks on the chopping block every day for the good of the United States. We should appreciate them. We should pray for them!

It brings tears to my eyes and upsets me terribly to think a president would reward Mr. Lawrence Summers by making him his director of economic council. And this came along with appointing another failure, Timothy Geithner, as his treasury secretary! Sean Hannity calls him a "tax cheat."[2] This gives me very little confidence that we are moving forward. It seems that they are throwing our freedom and future away by throwing trillions of dollars into the winds of Wall Street and to the corporate thieves of America.

I wonder if anyone has thought of investigating a conspiracy theory? It seems that some of them could be following a blueprint to force us into the new world order as soon as possible. Think about it: according to the polls in early September, President Obama was not going to be elected president. Then suddenly everything fell apart! The Wall Street jitterbug came up overnight! It seems like perfect timing; some would say so.

Maybe this would be a good time to reread chapter 14, "The Coming of a New World Order."

sixteen

OBAMA

MICHAEL STEELE, CHAIRMAN of the Republican Party, sent me my 2010 Republican National Convention Gold Card! I'm going to carry it with pride and with renewed purpose, knowing all this stuff I'm writing about is going to give all of us a fresh vision.

There are few things Michael Steele and others are zeroing in on concerning the Democratic Congress and Obama. Along with my Gold Card, Steele included this letter:

> President Obama and his Democratic allies in Congress are using this current economic crisis to accelerate their liberal agenda across the board. They are growing the size and scope of government at all levels, increasing spending to unrecoverable levels, changing the tax code to redistribute the wealth of working families and destroying the savings of millions of middle class Americans.
>
> Along with their allies in the liberal mainstream media, they have convinced a disturbing number of people that their huge spending plans and crushing tax burden on small businesses and individuals will grow the economy during a recession.
>
> The truth about President Obama and his cohorts, Nancy Pelosi and Harry Reid, is that they are hoodwinking American people into thinking their new spending and tax increases will be used to cut the federal deficit in half by 2013!

The facts are:

> The 2009 and 2010 Obama budgets would increase taxes by 1.4 trillion and increase the national debt to $23.1 trillion over the next ten years, stifling any hope of a quick economic recovery.
>
> The proposed cap and trade program on carbon emissions would impose at least $646 billion in

new energy taxes that will be paid by every American family as companies pass it on to consumers. [Can you imagine what this will do to your electric bill and gas bill?]

Even the Democrat's own Congressional Budget office said these estimates are optimistic on future revenue and economic turnaround—so the real deficits will be much higher.

The Republican Party would gladly work with the Democrats if their budget busting policies were not wrong for America.

The Republican reforms would give fast acting tax relief to boost the economy and create jobs, returning power to the people. They would have an immediate impact.

The Democrats' plan to let the Death Tax Zoom in 2011 from zero to fifty-five percent.

Despite Barack Obama's pledge to lead a government with highest standards of ethics, he has appointed more than twenty federal registered lobbyists to his administration!

He pledged he would give the public five days to examine any legislation passed by Congress before he signed it! He has broken every pledge repeatedly!

Taking advantage of the economic downturn which their party caused by forcing banks to give loans to unqualified buyers.....they have rammed through the largest, most wasteful piece of legislation ever! [Haste makes waste!]

To put this unprecedented level of public deficit in prospective, consider that Barack Obama, in a matter of weeks, has now inflicted more debt on the people of America than all his predecessors combined from George Washington on to George W. Bush.

If all the preceding was not enough, they have now, by public conversation about terrorist interrogations, aired our techniques to the world, including our enemies. [I remember back when something like this would be considered a form of treason or at the very least certainly unpatriotic!] The enemies have to be elated to hear that our interrogations will be ordered to properly heat their tea to correct temperatures before serving them!

Consider the following passage from William J. H. Boetcker:

You cannot bring about prosperity by discouraging thrift. You cannot strengthen the weak by weakening the strong. You cannot help small men by tearing down big men. You cannot help the poor by destroying the rich. You cannot lift the wage-earner by pulling down the wage-payer. You cannot keep out of trouble by spending more than your income. You cannot further the brotherhood of man by inciting class hatred. You cannot establish sound security on borrowed money. You cannot build character and courage by taking away a man's initiative and independence. You cannot help men permanently by doing for them what they could and should do for themselves.[1]

IS LIBERAL CONGRESS ASLEEP ON THE JOB?
BY MILTON F. MUSKEWITZ

In the first three months as president, the liberal Congress has stood by silently while Obama flagrantly breaks the law and tramples on our citizens' rights that we are accustomed to.

Obama has formed a partnership with the unions, who, with the help of ACORN, is his biggest source of votes. How can Obama justify browbeating the secured creditors of bankrupt Chrysler, forcing them to settle for pennies on the dollar, while giving fifty-three percent ownership of Chrysler to the union, an unsecured creditor.

In bankrupt situations, secured creditors always come first. It's the law.

Obama has taken the unheard of liberty of firing CEOs and dictating bonus and salary limits for private businesses such as banks, etc. Where is Congress? They are either asleep or willing accomplices. Obama criticized Bush for having a thirteen percent budget deficit, when in fact, come October, Obama's budget will have a fifty percent deficit, which relates to borrowing fifty percent of the budget dollars to finance his socialist agenda.

As deep in debt as Obama has put our country, now comes Obama's health care program for forty-five million people, fifteen million of them illegal aliens. Obama is operating a smoke and mirrors scheme which in time will destroy our health care system and bankrupt our country.

PRESIDENCY: A CASE OF DERELICTION OF DUTY?
BY MILTON F. MUSKEWITZ

Thank goodness for talk shows, Fox News, and the *Wall Street Journal*. Without them we would not have a clue as to the "obscene" efforts of Obama and his henchmen, including Congress and the "Czars," to take everyone's freedom away.

Unless you pay close attention, you won't realize how we are being victimized with higher taxes, the coming $120 billion reduction in Medicare payments, and his planned cut of $400 billion to doctors serving Medicare patients. Obama also will not address the tort reform since the lawyers are the second largest contributor to his campaign.

Obama made a deal with the drug companies to protect their profits in exchange for backing his health care program—politics as usual. How will this affect the seniors: higher taxes, higher out of pocket medical payments, and less quality of health care with the coming influx of added people to the health care program.

In his campaign speeches, he promised to tax the large corporation's earnings overseas. After a meeting with the "big boys," all of a sudden there will be no IRS expansion to collect overseas earnings, resulting in a possible $200 billion loss of collection of taxes each year. How about the IRS looking the other way and letting seniors off the tax hook?

Obama cancels a potential $200 billion taxable income, and yet is proposing to fine us if we don't carry health insurance.

Where is Obama exercising his duty as President? Our boys are dying in Afghanistan, due to his lack of leadership. How is it that he sits on his throne while the value of the dollar is sinking daily? All he has to do is tell the feds to raise interest rates. He is in bed with Wall Street and does not have a clue how to lower our 10 percent unemployment rate.

His answer is to extend unemployment benefits and print more money for another stimulus. I don't know if it is dereliction of duty, just plain stupidity— or is his *real* agenda to destroy America?

When you consider those that have given up or lost hope, the unemployment average across the country would be astounding!

President Obama, I have no problem with the color of your skin. I do mission work with people of all colors and faiths. I have never had a problem! My problem with you is your arrogance, your questionable patriotism, your ties to ACORN, your "radical czars," and more. More things are showing up even in your first eleven months! I quote a faithful black columnist, Star Parker, "He is not only our first black president, he is also our first president who doesn't like the free country he was elected to lead and feels his job is to change it. He has focused on warming up our relations with Islamic Nations and cooling down our Israeli ones."[2] (See this complete article in Section, "Let's Help the Jews Get Home.")

If J. C. Watts, black former Congressman from Oklahoma, continues to season properly, I would be honored to see him as president one day!

From reports from professionals, the general consensus is that the economy will probably get better for a short time. You, President Obama, will need to enjoy any credit for this, because it will get much worse within a couple of years since the Democrats have gone about this totally backwards. We will never be able to pay the debt. Experts are saying in all probability we will be bankrupt.

I say if things ever get better, it will be all from God's decision. Read 2 Chronicles 7:14. This is His prescription! Also, Acts 4:12 simply states, "There is no other name under heaven given to men by which we must be saved." Jesus' name, His love, His grace, His blood that flowed from Him on the cross at Calvary is the only way we can be saved. We do not even have a right to have real fellowship with the Father until we become His child. This is going to separate the men from the boys when we get desperate for God to heal our land!

I believe this needs to start at the top. We, as human Americans, like to follow our leader and take pride in doing what our peers do. That's why if you, Mr. President, ever decide this is the way to lead, let me know. I'll meet you any time, any place. We will pray through about this! I'll become your brother in Christ. I'll forgive you, and I'll hug your neck!

I pray God will have mercy on Obama, Harry Reid, Pelosi, Geithner, Lawrence Summers, and others that have apparently, in less than 365 days, lead our government to being broke financially.

Every president in my lifetime has come into the office with a positive attitude. Many presidents have come into office during a recession or at least an economic downturn. I believe the liberal public was supporting Obama and wanting him to lead the country instead of depending on God, the only true leader! The public had confidence in Obama that he could make things better until he started selling all of us on how bad things are. Now he is kind of admitting we're broke, knowing his team broke us! They have not delivered on anything he promised in the way of ethics, and so on.

This haste has created trillions of dollars of debt. No one even knows where a lot of the money has gone because there has been poor accounting.

Instead of keeping their eye on the ball, they have wanted to prosecute George Bush for allowing waterboarding of terrorists, while this is standard procedure in training some of our Navy personnel!

There are reportedly 9,287 earmarks in the omnibus stimulus bill, including $200,000 for a tattoo removal program, $1.8 million for manure management and "swine odor" research, $800,000 for "oyster rehabilitation," and $1.1 million for trapping mosquitoes, to name only a few.[3]

Reid has his own separate stimulus going on to the tune of $8 billion to be used for a high speed train rumored to be for carrying gamblers from Los Angeles to Las Vegas![4] Seems like this entire economic crisis has been deliberately exaggerated, with trillions of dollars being thrown up as into the winds!

This is what journalist Jay Ambrose has to say about the president's spending:

> This past year has been one of runaway, crazed political recklessness, we now face extraordinary dangers as a country, and President Obama gives no sign of planning to apply the brakes....
>
> Not that Obama is wholly responsible for the truly frightening rise in federal debt that we see.... But instead of addressing this debt crisis, he has exacerbated it, giving us an ineffectual, politically instructed stimulus package costing as much as the war in Iraq, for example, and working to ram a multi-trillion-dollar health plan down our throats.
>
> Despite applause from the left, this extravagance is worse than irresponsible.
>
> Considering that its chief objectives could have been achieved at virtually no additional costs and how it worsens our plight, it is insane.
>
> The latest warning about our peril comes from the Peterson-Pew Commission on Budget Reform, composed of 34 former government officials of both parties, people respected on both sides of the aisle. Here is their conclusion: With a total debt now at

$11.9 trillion, the worst could happen over time or immediately, such as buyers of Treasury securities demanding higher interest rates, a declining standard of living, lower wages and fewer safety nets.

The authors of the commission report agree that steep spending reductions before the recession has lifted might not be advisable, but do want a series of stabilizing steps to begin right away and to continue over the years to come…What's crucial are spending controls of the kind wholly anathema to our leftist leaders.

Obama and congressional Democrats talk as if they want to control health costs, for instance, but that's all it is—talk. There is absolutely no way the planned extension of health insurance through the various techniques they favor will decrease government health expenditures that are already a foremost cause of our budgetary mess.…

Obama wants more of the same while also subscribing to the notion that cap-and-trade will boost our economy and help control temperatures when, in fact, it could cost us a fortune and do next to nothing to control temperatures. There's at least this—2010 is [and future years are]…a chance to reverse policies.[5]

The next thing I expect to hear is the Democrats' team announcing to the world that the only way to go forward from here is to support some "world bank creation." Remember, the creation of a world bank is said to be part

1 of the new economic world order that has been foretold for years as a demonic Antichrist master plan. Phase 2 will be one world government, and phase 3 will be one world religion!

I'm so thankful I'm prepared and ready to go to heaven when God calls. It is my desire to take as many people with me as possible!

seventeen

THE LAST STEP OF THE LAST DAYS

Red, yellow, black, and white are all very precious in His sight! This is a small portion of the people we witnessed to at the edge of Cozumel, Mexico, utilizing an interpreter. This group grew to over one hundred people when we organized a New Work Church for them.

I N A TV program, I heard Pastor John Hagee ask the question, "Where are we in Bible prophecy?" Then he stated, "The last step of the last days!" He believes that very soon the world will be changing forever! The only thing that matters is whether you are saved. It is time to reign in your life. Pastor Hagee also states that God may be allowing this economic disorder as part of His plan!

I tend to agree with Pastor Hagee. Hagee and the

writings of other economists show there are strong signs that by the time the 2012 election comes around or soon thereafter, things could be so bad that some, even atheists, may jump from bridges, etc. Others will be ready to accept Christ as their Savior! Even some Democratic Congressional leaders will be ready to bow, according to 2 Chronicles 7:14.

I believe wake-up call after wake-up call has been unheeded, and God is, in a way, allowing Obama and his buds to further tear this nation apart economically. It appears the only thing that many folks notice is their pocketbook and bank accounts!

The story in 1 Kings 18 has a strong resemblance to and reminds me of what is occurring in America now. There was a great drought and famine in the land of Israel. The purpose was to give Ahab, an irrational king, an opportunity to repent. Ahab had been teaching the people that Baal was God and his wife, Jezebel, was taking care of 850 prophets of Baal and Asherah combined (v. 19). Ahab was the cause of national judgment; thus, the famine came and had lasted for three and one-half years. If he repented, rain would come!

Elijah decided that Israel had to choose who was God, the Lord or Baal. Then Israel had to serve God wholeheartedly. Rather than have them decide by his own message, Elijah sought a visible sign from heaven so all would believe. From Elijah's simple prayer, God sent enough fire to burn not only Elijah's sacrifice, but also twelve barrels of water. Then God sent the rain and ended the three and one-half years of drought and famine. When this happened on Mount Carmel, it should have settled this issue for all time.

It seems to me we need a modern-day Elijah to step up and get this issue settled again today.

When things get bad enough, many people will pray the "prescription prayer," 2 Chronicles 7:14, in desperation! They will bow and ask for His forgiveness. Will God heal our land if this takes place? God states at the end of this command that He will heal their land and forgive their sin. I believe most politicians will soon be afraid to stay in office or run for office unless they are believers.

I have no idea how this may take place or how long it will take, but I do believe real revival like we have never even dreamed of will take place all across the land.

The preceding, scenario 1, is the Christian dialogue of what we pray and hope for and what would be the best scenario for us all.

On the other hand, if the liberals stay in power, along with the liberal media, it seems they might be leading us toward the ushering in of the new world order as soon as possible. This is scenario 2. It could even be their main objective of why they are doing what they are doing!

Maybe they believe—as a large percentage of them must not be Christians—that the connection between a worldwide dictatorship and one world economic order is the ultimate plan. I wonder if any of them would admit to this. Remember their reaction to Senator Byran Dorgan, who saw it coming, trying to do the right thing and giving warning after warning?

Enough said! The decision may already be made. However, remember that the next time you vote for a president or congressman, you will be ultimately voting for scenario 1 or scenario 2. We may be closing in on America's biggest and fastest metamorphosis.

eighteen

FINALE

Photo credit: Dick Madden

THE LIGHTHOUSE

There's a Lighthouse on the hillside
that overlooks life's sea.
When I'm tossed it sends out a light
that I might see.
And the light that shines in the darkness,
now will safely lead us o'er.
If it wasn't for the lighthouse
that ship would be no more.

Everybody that lives around me says,
tear that lighthouse down,
The big ships don't sail this way anymore,
there's no use of it standing 'round.
Then my mind goes back to that stormy night,
when just in time I saw the light,
Yes, the light from that old lighthouse,
that stands up there on the hill.

And I thank God for the Lighthouse,
I owe my life to Him,
For Jesus is the Lighthouse,
and from the rocks of sin
He has shone a light around me
that I can clearly see,
If it wasn't for the Lighthouse
where would this ship be?*

ON THE COVER

Saint Marks, Florida, Lighthouse
Original Structure Completed in 1830

As we see this lighthouse in the likeness of the song, it ministers to me that its reflection shows it upside down in the water, presenting the message that some folks want to turn our heavenly Father upside down. To others it may show that our heavenly Father desires that we be a reflection of Him.

❧ 🔲 ❦

My oldest son, Tommy, is an ordained Southern Baptist minister in Lake City, Florida. He delivered the following sermon to our church on July 5, 2009. This is an important lesson for all of us who want to see God move and bless us, bless our nation, bless our homes and families.

---

* THE LIGHTHOUSE

Ronnie Hinson

© 1971 Songs Of Calvary Publishing (admin. by Dayspring Music, LLC), Dayspring Music, LLC

All Rights Reserved. Used By Permission.

Persistent Prayer
By Tommy Hudson

I believe God answers prayer. I believe He answers prayer in His time and in three ways: 1) yes, 2) no, and 3) wait. Waiting is sometimes the most difficult. You may be in God's waiting room right now.

Here's a question that may help us glean some truths and principles we can readily apply from God's Word. Our example will be the persistent widow referred to in the eighteenth chapter of Luke's Gospel, verses 1–8.

Why do I keep on praying even though I don't get an answer? Or maybe a better way to phrase this is, What do I do while I'm waiting for an answer? And the answer is: pray, pray, pray, because:

> 1) Persistent praying focuses my attention. (And that's Prayer Principle #1.) Romans 8:7–8 says, "Because the carnal mind is enmity against God: for it is not subject to the law of God, neither indeed can be. So then they that are in the flesh cannot please God" (KJV).

The word *enmity* discussed here means "deep-seated animosity" or "hatred." The apostle Paul declared in Rom. 8:7 that the human mind naturally has "enmity toward God," changed only through the redemptive power of Christ. Let me explain: "The heart is…desperately wicked: who can know it?" (Jer. 17:9, KJV)—the reason for murder and other heinous crimes. In our flesh and apart from God, who knows what we're capable of? Theologians refer to this as our Adamic nature. Since we inherited our sin nature from the first man, Adam, there must be a way, a remedy if you will, for us to be restored into relationship and sweet fellowship with God as He intended. Jesus is that remedy. The Old Testament remedy was an animal sacrifice and had to be done over and over. When Jesus came to Earth in the New Testament, He became the perfect, spotless Lamb and shed His blood as the permanent—once and for all—cure or remedy for sin. And remember, the Bible says without the shedding of blood there is no remission of sin. (See Hebrews 9:22.)

Human nature is to think we can handle any and everything on our own. My son, Brice, recently—just last week—had his third birthday. He tells me on a regular basis, "I can do it myself." However, my fatherly nature is to want to help him so he won't mess something up, get hurt, etc. As his father, I just feel like I know what is best for him. Sometimes it just makes my day to help him. The Creator of the universe is the same way with us. When we realize we're dependent on God's help (even to breathe), self decreases and God increases. Our attention focuses on Him.

2) Persistent praying clarifies my request. Philippians 4:6 says, "Be anxious for nothing,

> but in everything by prayer and supplication,
> with thanksgiving, let your requests be made
> known to God" (NKJV).

Has this ever happened to you? Someone comes to ask something of you; they talk and talk and talk, but at the end of the end of the talk you had to ask, "So what is it you're asking me to do?" Many times writing something, as in a journal, or speaking something aloud clarifies our thoughts. Our ideas become more clear to ourselves and communication is improved with others.

> 3) Persistent praying tests my faith. James
> 1:2–4 says, "My brethren, count it all joy
> when you fall into various trials, knowing that
> the testing of your faith produces patience.
> But let patience have its perfect work, that
> you may be perfect and complete, lacking
> nothing" (NKJV).

Sometimes prayer begins like this: "God, if you're really up there, then _____." (You fill in the blank.) Remember the story about the man who fell off the cliff and was sure to fall to certain death, except for the twig he grabbed on the way down? He called out and cried out, "Help! Is there anybody up there?" until eventually a voice from above shouted, "Just let go. You'll be OK." He thought for a second and cried out again, "Help! Is there anybody else up there?" He didn't realize there was a ledge a few inches down where he could safely rest and wait while the ultimate help plan was on the way. Isn't that the way we are with God when things don't happen in our timing? Remember, sometimes there is no testimony without a test.

> 4) Persistent praying prepares my heart for the answer. Ephesians 3:20 says, "Now to Him who is able to do exceedingly abundantly above all that we ask or think, according to the power that works in us, to Him be glory in the church by Christ Jesus to all generations, forever and ever. Amen" (NKJV).

When we're consistent in Principles 1, 2, and 3, the lines of communication are wide open, and so is our heart.

Our hearts are ready to receive, and we realize that Proverbs 3:5–6 in God's Word, which says, "Trust in the LORD with all thine heart; and lean not unto thine own understanding. In all thy ways acknowledge him, and he shall direct thy paths" (KJV), really means to trust in the Lord with all your heart and lean not on your own understanding; in all your ways acknowledge Him, and He will direct your paths.

Our hearts are ready to receive and we realize that Hebrews 13:5, which says, "I will never leave you nor forsake you" (NKJV), really means He will never leave you or forsake you.

Our hearts are ready to receive and we realize that Romans 8:28, which says, "And we know that all things work together for good to those who love

God, to those who are the called according to His purpose" (NKJV), really means, "And we know that all things work together for good to those who love God, to those who are the called according to His purpose."

And we could go on and on with these wonderful truths from God's Word.

We serve a wonderful Savior, and we must remember Jesus is forever on the throne, God is forever in control, and we are forever His children if we've personally accepted Jesus Christ as our Lord and Savior.

Below are verses used in sermon preparation and presentation:

Then He spoke a parable to them, that men always ought to pray and not lose heart, saying: "There was in a certain city a judge who did not fear God nor regard man. Now there was a widow in that city; and she came to him, saying, 'Get justice for me from my adversary.' And he would not for a while; but afterward he said within himself, 'Though I do not fear God nor regard man, yet because this widow troubles me I will avenge her, lest by her continual coming she weary me.'" Then the Lord said, "Hear what the unjust judge said. And shall God not avenge His own elect who cry out day and night to Him, though He bears long with them? I tell you that He will avenge them speedily. Nevertheless, when the Son of Man comes, will He really find faith on the earth?"

—Luke 18:1–8, nkjv

When we as heads of our households get serious and lead our families in this kind of fervent, persistent prayer, this will cause revival to break out in enough of our homes that it will spread like wild fire to our churches and other places of worship!

When we see this breakout in the majority of our homes and churches, it will travel to our state houses and to our White House. Then we will witness real change that you can believe in!

Perhaps we are a nation approaching judgment, and God has placed us here because He is unhappy with our country and wanting to give His children one more chance to get it right. Perhaps we as a country are at the place God intends for us to be, just like Jonah in the nasty belly of a whale. Jonah was a much quicker learner than some liberal folks in the USA. Jonah got serious with God and repented and changed his way of thinking and his life. We are lukewarm and being hurt by the actions of the liberals. This is so alarming to me because He gave us a quick fix/prescription of exactly what we need to do in 2 Chronicles 7:14.

It seems wake-up call after wake-up call, such as 9/11, has gone unheeded. I saw the beautiful towers less than one month before they exploded from terrorist attacks. Quite frankly their beauty was the thing I was most impressed with in New York, other than the Statue of Liberty, Times

Square, the Brooklyn Bridge, the Hudson River, and Central Park. I went back about three years ago to see basically nothing but a hole in the ground. I did take note of a street sign at the corner of the vacant hole. It was located at the corner of Trinity and Liberty Streets. This gave me more thoughts that God knew what He was doing, and perhaps He was telling us if we are to retain our liberties as a nation we are going to have to come back to the Trinity! This lack of progress at the site reminds me of the Tower of Babel story.

This also tells me we are at the crossroads of our lives, individually and as a country. You know a crossroads is an intersection at which you have to choose which way is the right way and which way you want to go. He gives us choices.

God bless America!

NOTES

INTRODUCTION

1. "9 Principles, 12 Values," The 9.12 Project, http://www
   .the912project.com/the-912-2/ (accessed December 3, 2009).
2. Ibid.
3. Deroy Murdock, "Oscar-Worthy Performance," *National Review,* February 16, 2007, http://article.nationalreview.
   com/?q=NmVlN2U5ZTc5ZTIyZjcxM2RjZjkxNjI2YzFiM2
   M5MmU= (accessed December 8, 2009).
4. Star Parker, "GOP Needs George Washingtons, Not Arlen
   Specters," WorldNetDaily (May 9, 2009), http://www.wnd
   .com/index.php?pageId=97488 (accessed December 3, 2009).

1—MY CURIOSITY WITH HOPE AND ITS LEADERS

1. Institute for the Study of American Evangelicals, "How
   Many Evangelicals Are There?" Wheaton College, http://
   isae.wheaton.edu/defining-evangelicalism/how-many
   -evangelicals-are-there/ (accessed December 3, 2009).
2. "About Us," Americans of Faith, http://www.operationvote.
   com/about.cfm (accessed December 3, 2009).
3. Mike Huckabee, *Do the Right Thing* (New York: Sentinel
   HC, 2008).
4. "Presidential Kittens" accessed at http://912member.
   blogspot.com/ (December 3, 2009).

2—PRESIDENT BILL CLINTON

1. All information in this timeline taken from the handout
   "A Brief Biography of President Bill Clinton," distributed
   by the Clinton Birthplace Foundation in Hope, Arkansas.

3—MIKE HUCKABEE: THE OTHER MAN FROM HOPE

1. "Biography," Mike Huckabee's Official Web site, http://www
.mikehuckabee.com/index.cfm?fa=Home.Biography (accessed
December 3, 2009).

2. Ibid.

3. Mike Huckabee, *Do the Right Thing*, Google Books,
http://books.google.com/books?id=uqnwwlaF3OwC&pg=P
A8&lpg=PA8&dq=We+have+to+give+voters+a+reason+to+c
hoose+us+as+guardians+of+their+future+huckabee&source
=bl&ots=s3V9jlrucx&sig=IaFBBnHS5raIivzriNpOY-NyctE
&hl=en&ei=mzAYS5jHJdWZlAehw5nnAg&sa=X&oi=bo
ok_result&ct=result&resnum=1&ved=0CAgQ6AEwAA#v
=onepage&q=guardians%20of%20their%20future&f=false
(accessed December 3, 2009).

4. Ibid.

5. Ibid.

4—PRESIDENT GEORGE W. BUSH

1. David Jackson, "First Lady Defends Bush's Record,"
USA Today, http://www.usatoday.com/news/nation/2008
-12-18-bush_N.htm?loc=interstitialskip (accessed December
3, 2009).

5—OPEN LETTER TO BLACK CONSERVATIVE CHRISTIANS

1. Star Parker, "When Color Trumps Christianity,"
Perspectives, http://www.onenewsnow.com/Perspectives/
Default.aspx?id=592920 (accessed December 4, 2009).

2. Quoted material taken from the Contemporary Christian
singer Carman's appearance on a Trinity Broadcasting
Network TV show.

3. "The Declaration of Independence," USHistory.org, http://www.ushistory.org/declaration/document/index.htm (accessed December 4, 2009).

7—SARAH PALIN, DOLLY PARTON, AND JIMMY CARTER

1. Wikipedia Online Dictionary, http://en.wikipedia.org/wiki/Independent_(voter) (accessed December 4, 2009), s.v. "Independent (voter)."
2. Mike Huckabee, "Fancy Nancy," *Press Room: Mike Huckabee*, http://www.mikehuckabee.com/index.cfm?fa=News.View&News_id=c371ff3b-a8f0-4b8d-a24c-0d0df1a0a047&Label_id=&Year=2009&Month=5 (accessed December 30, 2009).
3. Mike Evans, *Jimmy Carter: The Liberal Left and World Chaos* (Time Worthy Books, 2009).

8—TEA PARTIES

1. Judy Lowery, "Did T.E.A. Parties Achieve Goal?" *Lake City Reporter*, April 24, 2009.
2. Jay Ambrose, "Hurrah for Tea Parties," Scripps Howard News Service, April 19, 2009, http://www.koreatimes.co.kr/www/news/opinon/2009/11/160_43412.html (accessed December 7, 2009).

9—OBAMA'S PRAISE FOR TIM TEBOW AND THE GATORS

1. Bill Theobald, "Obama Praises Tebow, Gators," *USAToday*, April 24, 2009, http://www.usatoday.com/sports/college/football/sec/2009-04-23-florida-white-house_N.htm (accessed December 7, 2009).
2. Ibid.

10—THE IRAQ WAR

1. Deroy Murdock, "The Democrats' War," *National Review Online*, March 2, 2007, http://article.nationalreview.com/?q =ODBjNGVmNjVkMGQ0NWJkNGRhNjA3Y2FkYmM2 OWE4MWY= (accessed December 7, 2009).

11—FAIR TAX

1. Neal Boortz and John Linder, *The Fair Tax Book* (New York City: Harper Paperbacks, 2006).
2. John Cornyn, "April 15 Without Forms and Headaches," HumanEvents.com, April 14, 2006, http://www .humanevents.com/article.php?id=14060 (accessed December 7, 2009).
3. Randy Bishop, "Randy Bishop Reporting," *Trucks for Huck,* January 15, 2008, http://trucksforhuck.blogspot .com/ (accessed December 7, 2009).

12—FREEDOM OF CHOICE ACT

1. "Support Our Efforts," American Center for Law and Justice, https://www.aclj.org/Petition/Default.aspx?&ac=1& Zip=*Zip&sc=3267 (December 7, 2009).

13—LET'S HELP THE JEWS GET HOME

1. Star Parker, "Obama Foreign Policy Shows Change in Values," *ScrippsNews*, April 24, 2009, http://www .scrippsnews.com/node/42721 (accessed December 7, 2009).
2. "The Ant and the Grasshopper," posted by Rev. Austin Miles on November 30, 2009, The Christian Coalition of America, http://www.cc.org/blog/ant_and_grasshopper modern_version (accessed December 7, 2009).

14—THE COMING OF A NEW WORLD ORDER

1. Dr. Larry Bates, *The New Economic Disorder* (Lake Mary, FL: Excel Books, 2009.

2. Ibid.

3. Ibid.

15—THE SENATOR WHO SAW IT COMING

1. Eric Adelson, "The Senator Who Saw It Coming," *Newsweek*, April 13, 2009, http://www.newsweek.com/id/192468 (accessed December 7, 2009).

2. Sean Hannity, "Geithner Goes After Tax Cheats?" *Hannity's America*, FoxNews.com, March 11, 2009, http://www.foxnews.com/story/0,2933,508784,00.html (accessed December 7, 2009).

16—OBAMA

1. William J. H. Boetcker, quoted in Thomas F. Schwartz, "Other Misnomers," Illinois Historic Preservation Association, http://www.state.il.us/HPA/facsimiles.htm (accessed December 7, 2009).

2. Star Parker, "Obama Foreign Policy Shows Change in Values."

3. Brian M. Reidl, "Omnibus Spending Bill," *The Heritage Foundation*, March 2, 2009, http://www.heritage.org/Research/budget/wm2318.cfm (accessed December 8, 2009).

4. Sean Hannity, "Harry Reid's Train to Nowhere," *Hannity's America*, FoxNews.com, February 16, 2009, http://www.foxnews.com/story/0,2933,493628,00.html (accessed December 8, 2009).

5. Jay Ambrose, "The Coming Debt Crisis," *ScrippsNews*, December 24, 2009, http://scrippsnews.com/content/ambrose-coming-debt-crisis (accessed January 8, 2010).

TO CONTACT THE AUTHOR

Wayne T. Hudson, Sr., Author dba
Wayne T. Hudson Inc.
P.O. Box 2273
Lake City, FL 32056
www.ametamorphosis.com
wayne@familyfocus.us